To the sons of Light and daughters of Day.

"But friends, you're not in the dark, so how could you be taken off guard by any of this? You're sons of Light, daughters of Day. We live under wide open skies and know where we stand."

1 THESSALONIANS 5:4–5, THE MESSAGE

The Rock of Roseville
725 Vernon St., Roseville, CA
95678 U.S.A.

www.rockofroseville.org
www.rockspots.tv

Copyright © 2009 Francis Anfuso
Cover design by Hans Bennewitz

Unless otherwise indicated, all Scripture quotations are taken from the Holy Bible, New Living Translation, copyright © 1996, 2004, 2007 by the Tyndale House Foundation. Used by permission of Tyndale House Publishers, Inc., Carol Stream, Illinois 60188. All rights reserved.

Survey results from the book, "unChristian: What a New Generation Really Thinks about Christianity... and Why It Matters" by David Kinnaman and Gabe Lyons, was used with permission from The Barna Group, Ltd. www.barna.org.

ISBN:
10-: 0-9791957-8-0
13-: 978-0-9791957-8-5

2029
CHURCH OF THE FUTURE

FRANCIS ANFUSO

ACKNOWLEDGMENTS

"You can live without an eye... but not without a stomach."
1 CORINTHIANS 12:22—THE MESSAGE

There are many unseen parts of Christ's magnificent body that, though for the most part are invisible on Earth, are invaluable. It is to these hidden armor bearers that I want to express my deep appreciation. Like Jesus, they cover my mistakes, labor behind the scenes, selflessly using their invaluable gifts to prepare a feast for those who will read and listen.

During the writing stage some helped with editing and proofreading. Stephanie VanTassell has become an indispensable creative assistant. Like a master architect, she takes disjointed pieces and allows them to flow seamlessly as God intended. She accepts the high bar of excellence with grace, adding the heart of a prophetic intercessor to see beyond the page and, at times, even the age. Thank you, Stephanie.

After Stephanie and I have given it our best shot, it is then sent to Kathy Kunde, a dear friend with whom God miraculously linked Suzie and me. In 1993, her dear father and only brother were killed in a small plane accident. At that time, God brought us in contact with Kathy, her precious mother and sister, as well as other family members. I would have never thought that 15 years later, someone so divinely connected to my past would play such a strategic role in helping write a book about the future. Kathy is just sharp. Coupled with a deep maturity and a love for Jesus, she is the perfect complement to a book dealing with such a far-reaching topic. Kathy, thank you for the gift that you are, and the insight you have brought.

For the audio book, I thank my 'A' team. Once again, Tass Souza, born Tassajara Yamamoto Souza, heard every painful mistake, every cough and gaffe. With the kindness of a saint, he advised me about words misspoken, and even grammatical and conceptual faux pas everyone else missed. Then it was Randy Sundstedt and Caitlin LeBaron's turn to patiently listen to it all, artfully piecing together the audio book. Blessings on you all for being worthy representatives of Jesus!

To Dr. Kandee Mamula, grandmother to a generation, I give heartfelt thanks for contributing your expertise to the discussion questions. Your anointing to encourage and challenge people to grow more like Jesus affects everyone around you.

On the graphic side, we called upon the ever-edgy gift of "the man with the perfect disposition," who says, "no problem," even after midnight, and the tenth revision. Hans, you are a glowing son in the faith, of whom I am so proud.

I must not fail to acknowledge that much of this book has been written while skiing in the wake of the anointed worship leaders and intercessors from the International House of Prayer (IHOP) in Kansas City. Their online presence was invariably the spiritual underpinning of all that I wrote, lifting me to the very Throne of God. I will forever be indebted to this Gideon's band of nameless and faceless ones who daily pay the price so multitudes around the world may drink alongside them from the River of Life. They are truly sons of Light, and daughters of Day.

My heartfelt thanks goes to Betty Price for her last-minute assistance with formatting and references. You are an answer to prayer and your unique gift is much appreciated.

The final salutation goes to the queen of my life, the bride of my youth, the mother of my quiver, and the esteemed matriarch of now four grandchildren. Her insights are reserved for the most enigmatic of all questions. When raw common sense is needed, I hear the call, "Earth to Francis," and there she is, the crystal-clear, profoundly insightful mother-of-us-all. My dear Suzie, I know how much God loves me because He sent you to me. I will love and cherish you always.

Francis Anfuso
francis@rockofroseville.com

CONTENTS

Dedication *1*

Acknowledgments *4*

Contents *7*

Foreword *8*

Introduction *11*

1   Dying Church *15*

2   Authentic Church *41*

3   Accepting Church *65*

4   Transparent Church *97*

5   Discerning Church *123*

6   Supernatural Church *149*

7   Virtual Church *173*

8   Persecuted Church *195*

9   Eternal Church *225*

Addendum *251*

Recommendations *262*

FOREWORD

I love the word 'primordial'. It speaks of the original, the first. I think that's why I love Francis. He is one of the original Jesus people born again in that pristine Jesus movement from northern California without all the trappings of religion. It was, "Jesus loves me this I know—so let's love one another and live in community and make Jesus real to all the non-religious."

The first time I met Francis Anfuso was through his recording on evangelism. I think Francis was the original prayer-to-music CD producer. I listened to the Jesus movement preachers and their primordial cry on that CD for hours and it set me on fire.

The book you are about to read is a primordial call to another Jesus movement that marks Francis' clarion message. We have made the pristine into the pretend. This book is an elemental cry to return to the real. No hypocrisy; truth expressed through extravagant love to the outsider and the enemy.

Here Francis, my friend, meddles with pretense and calls us back to our first love. My life is one of a servant standing for truth in the public square, fasting and praying for the dislodging of demonic powers that release ideologies destructive to society. I find myself in the continuous challenge to make war in the heavens and carry a towel on the earth, washing the feet of those who would disagree and even rage against me. In the battle for truth we are pressed hard to not become like the beast we are trying to destroy.

Francis calls the Church to be oiled with love so that we may reveal the simplicity of the gospel in a hostile environment and reveal the original Jesus so the world can see Him. We're going back to the original, but only from the first things can we point to the future things. Francis always seems to be in front. This book calls us to see the future Church; what it must be and where it must go if it is to lead the parade of history in prayer and power.

The church Francis and Suzie planted was the first to encourage me to write a book. *Digging the Wells of Revival* was funded for publication by the people of The Rock of Roseville Church. That book was my primordial cry; a yearning for historic revival, even a Jesus movement like Francis was born in. What an encouragement to me. Like Barnabas of old, the original son of encouragement, Francis calls us into our destiny. With the sharpness of a surgeon's knife he cuts out the cancer and smokes out the phony. I think Jesus was like that. He was a man full of grace and truth. He was the primordial man; the one who was from the beginning. From Francis' life and from this book the Church may find herself going back to the future and experience afresh this man Jesus, the "man of steel and velvet."

Lou Engel
Co-Founder of The Call
www.TheCall.com

INTRODUCTION

"The man who views the world at 50 the same as he did at 20 has wasted 30 years of his life."

MUHAMMAD ALI

The future of Heaven and Earth is certain. God wins, the Devil loses, and mankind is divided.

Today, more than ever before, the church continues to be intrigued by increasingly obvious end time scenarios, daily unfolding for all those with discerning eyes to see. Since the first century, one primary question of the concerned church has been, "How close are we to the end?" We are captivated asking "when?" But the infinitely more important questions are, "What will the Church look like?" and "How can we become who God created us to be?" Helping the Church find the answers to these questions led me to write this book. Though, this is not the first time.

Twenty years ago when launching 21st Century Ministries, God gave me a clear vision for the church of the future. The outgrowth of this divine impression was a book entitled: We've Got a Future—The 21st Century Church.[1] I was so filled with prophetic unction, and so persuaded of the need within the church that my wife and I sold our home and put the equity into the project. We then spent two full years globetrotting the world, preparing others for what we sensed was ahead. We toured four nations and nearly 100 cities with a band, multi-media presentation, and a fervent vision. Many of those who viewed the presentation and read the book agreed. Some did not.

My family and I were impassioned to see a church modeled after the qualities outlined in the book. In 1997, we pioneered a church called The Rock of Roseville in Roseville, California. This healthy church prototype has grown to 2,000 people.

---

[1] Anfuso F. *We've Got A Future*—The 21st Century Church
(Sierra Madre, CA: 21st Century Ministries, 1989).

Now, two decades after its release, the entire book reads like a detailed depiction of the church of today. Amazingly, although many times tragically, 100 percent of the societal statistics in We've Got a Future have continued as projected. By the grace of God, almost none of its predictions have proven inaccurate.

Even reading it now, I'm still in agreement with its content. The following section and chapter titles from this book are still relevant for today. These titles provide a wholesome snapshot of what is still working within the contemporary church model. As you read them, it is worth noting that in 1989, some of these needful dimensions were far from evident to all.

WE'VE GOT A FUTURE:
THE 21ST CENTURY CHURCH CHAPTER AND SECTION TITLES

The Relatable Church
The Youthful Church
The Harvest is Always Young
The Creative Church
Yesterday's Heretics May Be Tomorrow's Heroes
If It's Boring, It's Probably Not of God
The Media Church
The Myth of Neutral Media
21st Century Daniels
Prayer and Fasting
Character vs. Charisma
The "Love" Movement
The Mission Fields of Tomorrow

At the time We've Got a Future arrived on the church scene, some thought the book was a premature Hail Mary Pass—provocative but not necessarily how the script would play out. Now 20 years later, it is still a valid benchmark of where the church was headed.

But that was yesterday's struggle. Today's battle is far more complex and will stretch us further than we ever imagined. The dramatic challenges of this hour are so obvious one hardly needs a futuristic or prophetic gifting to interpret the handwriting on the wall. What is needed however is the solution.

Though I launch this futuristic sequel with an appropriate measure of concern, I am convinced of its direction. I'm betting my life on it. Time will tell.

This is a long distance call. It will cost you much to answer it. God designed all of our tomorrows to be better than today. What they look like is incidental. How we walk them out is essential.

May we build wisely, or those who follow us will find themselves unprotected and unprepared for the dangers we should have seen. Now is the time for the Church to be all God intended. Now is the time for every follower of Jesus to BE the Church.

Francis Anfuso, August 2009
Take a look at where we are today at:
www.rockofroseville.com
www.rockspots.tv

A "chronologically updated" version of We've Got a Future— The 21st Century Church is free to read online at www.futurechurchupdate.com

DYING CHURCH

CHAPTER ONE

"My aim is to know Him, to experience the power of His resurrection, to share in His sufferings, and to be like Him in His death, and so, somehow, to attain to the resurrection from the dead."

THE APOSTLE PAUL PHILIPPIANS 3:10–11 (NET)

The Church in the Western World is dying.

Much of her languishes somewhere between the religion of her parents and the rebellion of her children. She strives for relevance while clinging to comfort. And all this straining of ideals is occurring in an age like none other.

There is a shaking of all that can be shaken. But it has only just begun.

In the next 20 years, the Church will face unprecedented challenges. Simultaneously, we will rise to overcome, empowered by the Spirit of God and fully transformed.

The Church in the Western World might be dying. But like Lazarus of old, the God of resurrection is waiting until it stinks to spring new life from the ground.[1]

Not long now.

---

1 John 11:39

> **The Church's rebirth is already growing in the hearts of millions of single-minded disciples of Jesus Christ.**

The Church's rebirth is already growing in the hearts of millions of single-minded disciples of Jesus Christ. We feel an urgency that cannot be fully articulated. This holy discontent is like the grain of sand irritating the oyster. We can spit it out in denial, or nurture what God has purposefully planted in us, accepting that the Church and life as a follower of Jesus will never be the same.

How do I know this? The Living God, the Creator of all things, made His promise clear and will not fail: "Christ's love makes the church whole. His words evoke her beauty. Everything He does and says is designed to bring the best out of her, dressing her in dazzling white silk, radiant with holiness."[2]

What changes will the Church experience in the next 20 years? How will she be perfected into Christ-likeness? What unique role do you have in this age?

In the next eight chapters, we will discover our great destiny as the Church of the Living God.

But for the bride to dress herself in dazzling white, she must first take off her rags and put away former things.

New life is coming—but death must happen first.

---

2 Ephesians 5:26-27, The Message

CULTURE WARS

"Don't copy the behavior and customs of this world, but let God transform you into a new person by changing the way you think."
ROMANS 12:2A

One culture colliding with another always signals change.

America is a country of immigrants who brought individual customs and traditions from their native lands. Over time, one group affected another until our nation was shaped into a unique world culture. Now, assimilation is so complete, it's difficult to see distinct differences between heritages.

Assimilation is defined as, "The process whereby a minority group gradually adopts the customs and attitudes of the prevailing culture."[3] While this can be construed as a positive contributing factor to the unity and success of the United States, it is detrimental to citizens of Heaven.[4]

When one culture collides with another, there will always be change. The question is, who's changing when Christ-followers collide with the world?

Jesus tells us that all the powers of hell will not conquer His Church.[5] We might be the minority, but that is no excuse to not be overcomers.

Have you ever noticed that where the grass is lush and green in your lawn there are no weeds; whereas, where there is no grass the weeds take over? One way to deal with the problem is to pull the weeds up when you see them, but that's a temporary and generally ineffective solution. Invariably, the weeds will grow back.

---

[3] *The American Heritage Dictionary of the English Language, Fourth Edition* (Houghton Mifflin Company, 2004).

[4] Philippians 3:20

[5] Matthew 16:18

But if you keep your grass as healthy as possible, over time it will displace most of the weeds. The cure for weeds is healthy grass.

In the spiritual realm, if I can cultivate a healthy relationship with God, virtue will weed out vice; the power of the Word will overcome the temptations of the world. The goal for the healthy person, family and church must be to saturate our lives with the Holy Spirit and the Word of God. "Don't let evil conquer you, but conquer evil by doing good."[6]

Now is the time to ask, where have we, the Church, been assimilated into the customs of this world? Where should we have been agents of transformation instead? In essence, where have weeds choked out healthy grass?

Today's culture is utilitarian, information-indulged, self-centered, apathetic, compromising and just plain bored. Many of these traits have spread from the public to the pews.

It's time they were weeded out, killed off once and for all.

THE DEATH OF UTILITARIANISM

In my youth I was an ethical hedonist.

I believed actions were right or wrong based upon the amount of pleasure they produced. The only pleasure that was immoral was that which hurt someone else. If it was to my benefit, or seemed to be, and didn't directly harm others, then my actions were no one's business.

It's my life, my choice; live and let live; I am accountable to no one but myself.

Utilitarianism, or as I refer to it, *You-tilitarianism*, places man at the center of all decisions. It presumes that we determine the

---

[6] Romans 12:21

value, worth, and moral relevance of every action. Our obsession with *In Humans We Trust* will eventually lead to bitter disappointment and regret.

During my own hedonistic reign of personal indulgence, I lured many a pleasure-seeker to dig a bottomless pit of un-fulfillment alongside me. I still bear the scars of this foolishness. Its inevitable result was allowing the devil to have his way.

We must learn to resist the temptation of being recast into the image of a flawed culture that has lost much of its eternal uniqueness.

This self-absorbed attitude has permeated the corrupt core of every culture since the beginning of time. It is the epicenter of our sin nature and the centerpiece of a wave of deception seeking to deform God's Church on Earth. Without divine intervention, it would be the undoing of both. But, thank God, He has written a script with a far more illustrious ending.

I have since learned to die to the "me-fixation," retaining my true identity and destiny. I was created in the image and likeness of God, and to Him I am first and foremost accountable—not to myself. My uniqueness and value come from God alone. If I lose touch with His original design for me, no other imagined intent can ever satisfy who I was created to be. So too are the promise and present danger for individuals, families and churches.

Aristotle once mused, "the whole is more than the sum of its parts." Though this is no doubt true, a more meaningful line would be, "the whole can be no more pure than the purity of its parts," or as the Bible says it, "a little yeast…spreads through the whole batch of dough."[7]

Your purity, your death to self, your surrender to the plans of God make an eternal difference and impact on the Kingdom of God.

---

7 Galatians 5:9

The math is always the same:

A little lie will subvert any truth; a little compromise will destroy any life, family or church. In this progressively precarious age the seduction of misrepresentation will only increase. We must learn to resist the temptation of being recast into the image of a flawed culture that has lost much of its eternal uniqueness.

We can know the future God has for us if we are willing to examine all we were, are, and hope to be in the light of God's incomparable thoughts—His Holy Word.

Consider this an invitation to open yourself up to God's comforting correction.

We must have the courage to hear and obey His admonishing whisper and not be intimidated by the shouts of the mangled mob. Only then can we show a skeptical world God's incomparable love and care for them. Then they will see He has done everything in His power to rescue and transform their lives as well.[8]

FEASTING SENSES—FAMISHED SOULS

"Of all the things I've lost, I miss my mind the most."
MARK TWAIN[9]

This has been called the "Information Age." Technological innovations, immediate updates via the internet, and a constant stream of television and radio content have made this the most informed era to date.

---

8 Psalm 23:4

9 Mark Twain quote. ThinkExist. Available at http://thinkexist.com/quotation/of_all_the_things_i-ve_lost-i_miss_my_mind_the/161541.html. Last accessed July 15, 2009.

But devouring an endless flow of data has made us none the wiser. Though the Bible predicted this increase of knowledge thousands of years ago,[10] more information has yet to produce greater insight. Suffocating under an avalanche of spiritual, ideological and moral opinions, God's Word discerns our dilemma: "Knowledge puffs up, but love builds up."[11] Similarly, knowledge may swell our heads but shrink our hearts. The knowledge of God and His truth alone bring eternal bliss.

Only God, the Author of life, can build a life worth living.[12] Unless we allow Him to be Lord, the insignificant fascinations of Earth will eventually possess us. It has been comically noted, "We used to build civilizations. Now we build shopping malls."[13] How many civilizations have come and gone, replicating this same foolish pattern? None of us are immune to its tragic consequence. And the exchange has not been worth it.

"In place of truth, we have discovered facts. For moral absolutes, we have substituted moral ambiguity," said Ted Koppel, of ABC's Nightline, at a Duke University graduation ceremony. He continued, "We have reconstructed the Tower of Babel, and it is a television antenna: a thousand voices producing a daily parody of democracy, in which everyone's opinion is afforded equal weight, regardless of substance or merit. Our society finds truth too strong a medicine to digest undiluted. In its purest form, truth is not a polite tap on the shoulder. It is a howling reproach. What Moses brought down from Mt. Sinai were not Ten Suggestions. They are Ten Commandments."

It seems no matter how much we drink, we just can't quench our thirst. McDonald's sodas are 42 ounces and growing. In 1955, when McDonald's was founded, the largest drink it offered its customers was seven ounces.

---

10 Daniel 12:4

11 1Corinthians 8:1b

12 Acts 3:15

13 Bill Bryson quote. Goodreads. Available at http://www.goodreads.com/quotes/show/13092. Last accessed July 15, 2009.

> **Unless we allow God to renew our hearts and minds we will spend our lives rummaging through the clutter of past pain, bound to cadavers of disappointment.**

Truth has no substitute. Without consuming the living water that leads to life,[14] we will eventually drown in an ocean of facts.

This isn't to say that the Church should shut off the mind in order to have life in the Spirit. On the contrary. We are called to love God with all our minds,[15] but there must also be a death to "every proud argument that keeps people from knowing God." We are called to "conquer their rebellious ideas," and to "teach them to obey Christ."[16]

Unless we allow God to renew our hearts and minds we will spend our lives rummaging through the clutter of past pain, bound to cadavers of disappointment. Jesus died and rose again so that death would no longer have authority over our lives. "Christ's one act of righteousness brings a right relationship with God and new life for everyone."[17]

As we physically wash ourselves each day, before and after being out in the world, God's Word challenges us to "…let the Spirit renew your thoughts and attitudes."[18] Draw a line in the sand of your heart. Refuse to allow the world, your flesh, or the devil to diminish your destiny. God's promise is that "…despite all these things, overwhelming victory is ours through Christ, who loved us."[19]

---

14 John 4:10
15 Deuteronomy 10:12
16 2Corinthians 10:4-5
17 Romans 5:18b
18 Ephesians 4:23
19 Romans 8:37

THE DEATH OF SELF-LOVE

Jesus spoke in absolute terms. "You must love the LORD your God with all your heart, all your soul, and all your mind."[20] The road to success for individuals, families and churches in the future will not be achieved by the fleeting fixation on self. It will be found by fully focusing our hearts, minds, and strengths upon the only true Savior meriting such adulation.[21]

Self-love often evolves into self-hatred.

Since we were not designed to esteem ourselves above God, or anyone else for that matter, this form of idolatry is considered the greatest of all sins. In the first of the Ten Commandments, the Lord emphatically states, "You must not have any other god but Me."[22] His warning is most certainly directed toward all people, at all times, for all generations. There are no exceptions!

> **The cultural ideal of "finding ourselves" is not the solution; it's actually the beginning of assessing the very nature of the problem.**

The cultural ideal of "finding ourselves" is not the solution; it's actually the beginning of assessing the very nature of the problem. "For everyone has sinned; we all fall short of God's glorious standard."[23]

One of the great shocks awaiting those who have spent their lives devouring the devil's assorted delicacies will be realizing that, after all the bravado and boasting, Satan has been rendered eternally impotent since the fall of man. All of the "father of lies" egocentric schemes went bust, as will the dreams of his shareholders.

---

20 Matthew 22:37

21 Mark 12:30, Luke 10:27

22 Exodus 20:3

23 Romans 3:23

Having resisted God's heart until the bitter end, hell's inhabitants will reap the consequences of their actions by choosing, sometimes unknowingly, eternal isolation instead of God's loving intention. They've chosen slavery over the inheritance of privileged sons and daughters of the Creator. All for one reason: self-willed man vainly insists on attempting to make himself a god.

We deny it. But instant-replay will reveal the truth. We want our own way, even if it ends in destruction, thinking we at least had the privilege of being behind the wheel. Claiming a supreme right to "freedom," this inane insurgency is anything but free. We are all soon entrapped in a depressing web of distraction, addiction and depression.

In contrast, God's plan is not the ranting of some eccentric egomaniac itching for the lead role in His own movie. He IS the epicenter of all life! "For in Him we live and move and exist."[24] What life can we live without the Author of life?

Only God can "play God." It is casting at its best.

How vastly different is Satan's destiny? Welcomed into everlasting damnation, he was met with a mocking cheer from hell's inhabitants. The Bible recounts this cynical ovation in chilling detail: "In the place of the dead there is excitement over your arrival. The spirits of world leaders and mighty kings long dead stand up to see you. With one voice they all cry out, 'Now you are as weak as we are! Your might and power were buried with you. The sound of the harp in your palace has ceased. Now maggots are your sheet, and worms your blanket.'"[25] It sounds like this alternate ending wasn't quite what Satan expected.

---

24 Acts 17:28

25 Isaiah 14:9–11

Thank God His original finale, the best of all options, is still lined up. Our merciful Creator refuses to live in denial. God knows the facts of life: He rules, and we can too, if we accept our supporting role in the greatest story of all time.

While there is still time, reinvest your heart, mind, soul and strength in the role you were created for.

Satan's audition as "God" totally bombed. The senior worship leader in Heaven read too many of his own press releases and never met a mirror he didn't like. The critics weren't impressed. Now he's stuck reliving his despicable role as the greatest oppressor of all time.

Now, prior to the devil's imminent final departure, he continues to entice the naïve to perform in the same ill-fated version of his really bad play. It's an encore performance of the same shallow lines first recited so very long ago. Adam and Eve were promised by the serpent, "You won't die! …God knows that your eyes will be opened as soon as you eat it, and you will be like God, knowing both good and evil."[26]

The queue stretches around the world to be cast in this tragedy.

While there is still time, reinvest your heart, mind, soul and strength in the role you were created for. You are a worshipper of the Living God!

The enemy of our souls has never had the ability to produce anything of eternal consequence. His only shot is to neuter the destinies of as many hapless victims as possible. Once lured down this same eternally barren road, they too will finish utterly alone, filled with regret, having missed the entire essence of life.

Officiating his own coronation as "god," Satan offers a worthless diploma to those naïve enough to exchange their true identity as "chosen of God" for the counterfeit, denying their God-given birthright.

---

26 Genesis 3:4–5

There is only one Creator and Sustainer of life from whom all things have come and to whom we will all return.[27] Though I refer to God as "He," the Almighty personifies all of the eternal male and female personality traits. In His very nature, He combines all of the marvelous qualities He Himself placed in men and women as an extension of Himself.

The very nature of reproduction is that it must involve more than just me. "I" did not produce my children or anything of lasting consequence. My lineage started long before my parents. My ancestors trace back to Noah and his wife, even to Adam and Eve (I'm actually an "Eden-American"). We are all created by God and for God. We will each give an account to Him for the life and stewardships we have been given.

Contrary to popular presumption, one of our planet's greatest challenges is not an over-abundance of inhabitants. If resources were allocated properly, we would have enough for all people for as much time as God has allotted us in this age. The central root of our dilemma is not too many people, but too few people relationally connected to our Creator, the Author and Finisher of life.[28]

With an infinitely greater capacity than any frail human institution, the God of the Universe longs to guide us by His Spirit through the challenging seasons ahead. He has promised to make provision for us regardless of the economic or ecological woes facing the planet. "And this same God who takes care of me will supply all your needs from His glorious riches, which have been given to us in Christ Jesus."[29]

---

[27] Colossians 1:17

[28] Hebrews 12:2

[29] Philippians 4:19

When we give up our responsibility to be fruitful and multiply[30] and, even more tragically, cut short the lives of those we propagate,[31] we rob our future by stealing from our present. Selfish motives will never bear the honorable fruit that values every life at every stage.

THE AGE OF HALF-LIFE

The term "half-life" is used in science, marketing, and finance. In science it is the amount of time it takes for a specific substance to decay to half of its potency, while in finance it is the amount of time it takes for half of your mortgage principal to be paid off.

Half-life for the Christian could be thought of as the amount of time it takes to become half as zealous for God or half as conscious of our value to a madly-in-love Creator. Over the years I've seen people digress to a spiritual half-life in months, weeks, and even days. It's chilling to watch, and is increasing its insidious effect as a blanket of deception attempts to smother the Western World.

The primary way God communicates with us is through His Word.

Tragically, many who claim to be followers of Jesus have lost touch with Him.

The primary way God communicates with us is through His Word. Out of 95 million Americans who are ages 18 to 41, about 60 million say they have already made a commitment to Jesus that is still important; however, only about 3 million of them have a biblical worldview.[32]

---

30 Genesis 1:28

31 Matthew 18:10

32 Kinnaman D, Lyons G. *unChristian: What a New Generation Really Thinks about Christianity... and Why It Matters* (Baker Books, 2007). www.barna.org

A biblical worldview means they believe the following eight truths:

1. Jesus Christ lived a sinless life.
2. God is the all-powerful and all-knowing Creator of the universe and He still rules it today.
3. Salvation is a gift from God and cannot be earned.
4. Satan is real.
5. A follower of Jesus has a responsibility to share his or her faith in Christ with other people.
6. The Bible is accurate in all of the principles it teaches.
7. Unchanging moral truth exists.
8. The Bible defines moral truth.

The root cause of this global malaise can be easily isolated: It is the end result of wanting things our own way.

Research shows that people who embrace these eight biblical beliefs live a substantially different faith from other Americans—even other believers. Unless our relationship with God is based upon His Word, we will eventually live in our own strength and move further away from God's plan for our lives.

Trying to preserve our future in our own strength will protect us about as well as a Kamikaze pilot wearing a helmet. Crash-and-burn is the inevitable consequence of self-delusion. Having lost our dependency upon God as Savior, the only eternal guarantee, much of the planet is lost in the maze of attempting to save ourselves. It is a role we are incapable of filling.

The root cause of this global malaise can be easily isolated: It is the end result of wanting things our own way. It always leads to frustration and confusion. These are the bitter fruits of being disconnected from our Creator, the source of life, liberty and true happiness.

Perhaps this is why Harrison Ford confessed, "I don't think I've mastered anything. I'm still wrestling with the same frustrations, the same issues, and the same problems as I always did. That's what life is like."[33]

Though there may be a thread of truth in this candid admission, it's frankly not what my life is like, and it's certainly not how God intended life to be. The Bible's guarantee of personal fulfillment is implicit and breathtaking: "…anyone who belongs to Christ has become a new person. The old life is gone; a new life has begun!"[34] Pinch yourself. This promise is for you!

Thankfully, I am not wrestling with the same frustrations, issues, and problems I always have. In countless ways, Jesus has healed my frustration, settled my issues and answered my problems. I am living an eternally grateful and blessed life beyond my wildest dreams.

My heart sincerely goes out to anyone who isn't. I can empathize with them, cry with them, and certainly understand the pain most people endure, day after day, year after year. But to say it is normal, healthy and our inevitable lot in life—no. I will not concede this! Jesus died so I don't have to live at half-life. Each day I awake to fully receive what He accomplished on my behalf. It allows me to live a life filled with gratitude and appreciation for who God is and all He does on my behalf.

I will grant that it is a full-court press to believe such an extraordinary truth. It is a daily battle for each of us to reject the lies of the enemy of our soul and to consciously embrace the promises Jesus died to give us. But, they are ours and we must fight to remain free! "He (God) has given us great and precious promises. These are the promises that enable you

It is a daily battle for each of us to reject the lies of the enemy of our soul and to consciously embrace the promises Jesus died to give us.

---

33 Harrison Ford quote. Westlord.com. Available at http://www.westlord.com/harrison-ford/quotes.html. Last accessed July 15, 2009.

34 2Corinthians 5:17

to share His divine nature and escape the world's corruption caused by human desires."[35]

Living beneath my potential would not be a novel experience. I spent years doing just that. As a suicidal, atheistic God-hater with a doctorate in depression, I offered free timeshares to Death Valley. I fully accept the fact that I will always be a work-in-progress. But my gracious God never intended my life to be a morbid, emotionally distraught marathon, watching endless re-runs of past frustrations, issues, and problems. As Paul the Apostle so humbly shared, "I don't mean to say that I have already achieved these things or that I have already reached perfection. But I press on to possess that perfection for which Christ Jesus first possessed me."[36]

Like Paul, I planted the seeds of obedience decades ago and they have grown into healthy emotional limbs that shade me from many of the uncertainties of life. I now take shelter and rest under God's constant care. Either we learn to yield our fragile hearts to the only One capable of fulfilling our lives, or we will eventually eat the bitter fruit of self-indulgence.

Becoming "all things to all men,"[37] doesn't mean I have to remain lost in the seeming meaninglessness of life in order to relate to the masses. I stand on the reality that the Lover of my soul has rescued me from the despondency of disconnection.[38] I have reclaimed much that was lost during my childhood and the many years of not having a personal relationship with God.[39]

The half-life of discomfort and uneasiness is gone. I am eternally grateful. If you can believe it, this has always been God's perfect plan for every person, family and church, both now and for all time. As you gaze into the future, may it be with

---

[35] 2Peter 1:4

[36] Philippians 3:12

[37] 1Corinthians 9:22

[38] Song of Solomon 2:3, 8–10, 16; 3:1; 5:1–2, 4, 6, 8–10, 16; 6:1–3; 7:13; 8:5,10

[39] Romans 8:28, 1Kings 8:56

a confident awareness that God is fully able "to accomplish infinitely more than we might ask or think."[40]

"...for I know the One in whom I trust, and I am sure that He is able to guard what I have entrusted to Him until the day of His return."[41]

"Now may the God of peace make you holy in every way and may your whole spirit and soul and body be kept blameless until our Lord Jesus Christ comes again. God will make this happen, for He who calls you is faithful."[42]

TERMINAL STILLNESS

There is constant movement around the mighty Throne of God. The River of Life with its healing properties flows continuously.

The ecstatic praise of blissful multitudes endlessly ascends toward the Father, saturating the atmosphere with His presence. We need to remind ourselves that the mountain-moving intercessory prayers of Jesus are ever-descending on Earth. All exist to serve the divine dream; actively engaged and marvelously fulfilled in living fully surrendered lives. So, what is the desperate need of Earth?

We need to remind ourselves that the mountain-moving intercessory prayers of Jesus are ever-descending on Earth.

Heaven must come!

If Jesus lives in us, then our longing for God is a longing for Heaven to come to Earth. If we have Heaven in us, then Heaven can come to any room we enter. If Jesus is in us, then we are even commissioned to lift every room we are in to Heaven

---

40 Ephesians 3:20b

41 2Timothy 1:12b

42 1Thessalonians 5:23–24

or to bring Heaven down. Jesus said, "…the kingdom of God (Heaven) is within you."[43] It is unmistakable!

When was the last time you invited Heaven to visit?

What causes God's heart to break in Heaven? I believe it is the disengagement of Earth; Heaven's one-sided dance without Earth as its partner. This terminal stillness of God's future bride leaves the groom waiting at the altar, longing for His betrothed to come and join Him, to bask in the presence of the Father while simultaneously reaching out to those who are yet to know His love.

We can break the static cycle of dead religion, and move Heaven and Earth in ecstatic worship by our obedience. Missing this opportunity is tragic, even a disgrace. The Book of Proverbs doesn't mince words when it throws down the gauntlet, "…one who sleeps during harvest is a disgrace."[44]

We will miss the cherished meaning of the moment if we are restrained by the limitations of Earth.

Let Heaven come!

Let it blast away the cobwebs of ritual Earth, with a fresh breeze!

Without our celestial partnership with God's Holy Spirit, without our impassioned cooperation with Jesus as our co-laborer and joint heir, we will idle away our precious time on Earth, missing the entire point of our existence.

"…for Thy pleasure they are and were created."[45]

Anything less than God's original intention will rob each of us of the glorious opportunity of both being fulfilled and fulfilling our privileged destiny in Him.

---

[43] Luke 17:21

[44] Proverbs 10:5

[45] Revelation 4:11, KJV

THE POSITIVE VALUE OF "NO"

We've all had a love-hate relationship with the word "No." But it is "No," as much as "Yes," that keeps the world on track.

As painful as "No" may be, it can be a lifesaver. If we don't learn how to say "No," we'll eventually lose our ability to say, "Yes" to all that is eternal and good. Ask any addict, boss, or good parent and they'll tell you that "No" can be the difference between life and death.

Mark Twain astutely quipped, "A banker is a fellow who lends you his umbrella when the sun is shining, but wants it back the minute it begins to rain."[46] But it is unregulated banks that cause the most pain. How many banks defaulted because they refused to say, "No"? "No" to greed, "No" to unethical or unwise shortcuts, even "No" to customers if an individual request was detrimental to the greater good. At times, no amount of "Yes's" can undo the damage done by a missed opportunity to say, "No."

> **If we don't learn how to say "No," we'll eventually lose our ability to say, "Yes" to all that is eternal and good.**

In my own life, I wish I'd said, "No" sooner and more often. In my youth, a swift "No" would have made the difference between moral purity and promiscuity. A courageous "No" would have avoided two abortions. An unwavering "No" would have caused the devil to get lost[47] and opened the door for the heart of God to be found, sooner than later.

Unless we learn to say, "No" to the world, our flesh, and the devil, we will eventually be overwhelmed by the seductive power of their combined "Yes." This is one of our essential strategies as individuals, families and churches in order to flourish in the uncertain days ahead.

---

46 Mark Twain quote. The Quotations Page. Available at http://www.quotationspage.com/quote/169.html. Last accessed July 15, 2009.

47 James 4:7

The Book of Judges tells the account of an evil general who sought a drink and a hiding place in the tent of a fearless and righteous woman.[48] She did as he requested. She gave him a drink and covered him up, but while he slept she drove a tent peg through his temple. Good for her.

As you read on, you may realize you have, in some way, allowed the enemy to come into your own tent to set up camp in your heart. Too many people have allowed the enemy into their tents. Having lost their ability to say, "No," they eventually give him full reign over their lives.

Kill him quickly!

Drive him out, or you will die with him.

Drive him out before he convinces you his motive is as good as God's.

SHAKING THE EARTH, STIRRING THE BRIDE

Have any of us missed how incredibly fragile our planet is?

Has it escaped our attention how little control we have over our economic future; that economists can't fix our fiscal problems; that politicians are unable to calm the storms? Continuing to put hope in our financial plans, our business ingenuity, or our monetary expertise is futile.

Even though much of the world is stressed out, irritable, fatigued, sleepless and angry, the culture will always tell you to put your hope in man's ability and on this life. That's all they know. It's all they have. No wonder so many people feel hopeless during unstable times. Their hopes are based on empty desire rather than on dependable destiny.

---

[48] Judges 4

In the spirit-realm, the spread of Islam around the globe could be the most threatening challenge to the Christian faith we presently face. According to the current population growth in Europe, by the year 2050, many of Europe's 31 nations will be Islamic Republics. The future growth and even survival of the Christian church in Europe will depend upon a revival of the genuine and life-giving Christian faith.

Without a move of God's Spirit, Europe will be essentially lost.

Across the entire European Union of 31 countries, the fertility rate is down but the population is up. How is this possible? Of all the population growth in Europe since 1990, 90 percent is Islamic immigration.[49]

One chilling quote predicting the demise of ethnic Germany came from none other than the German government. "The fall in the German population can no longer be stopped. Its downward spiral is no longer reversible."[50]

The only hope for planet Earth is Jesus, the living Word of God.

Unless our future hope is in trusting and obeying God's Word, we have no future. It is just wishful thinking! This presumptuous perspective of placing our hope in ourselves has happened over and over again since the beginning of time.

Some examples are recorded in the Old Testament. In the Book of Haggai, for example, around 520 BC, a remnant of the nation of Israel had returned from being held captive in Babylon (modern day Iraq) for 70 years. It was 16 years after their return to Jerusalem. They had primarily focused on rebuilding their own lives and not the walls of the city or the Hebrew Temple. The

> **Unless our future hope is in trusting and obeying God's Word, we have no future. It is just wishful thinking!**

---

49 Williamson R. *Global Jihad: Lifting the Veil of Islam* (These Last Days Ministries, 2009).

50 German Federal Statistics Office. Nov. 7, 2006.

prophet Haggai admonished them about their priorities at a critical time:

> "This is what the Lord of Heaven's armies says: look at what's happening to you! You have planted much but harvest little. You eat but are not satisfied. You drink but are still thirsty. You put on clothes but cannot keep warm. Your wages disappear as though you were putting them in pockets filled with holes! This is what the Lord of Heaven's armies says: look at what's happening to you! Now go up into the hills, bring down timber, and rebuild My house. Then I will take pleasure in it and be honored, says the Lord."[51]

God is always trying to get our attention. He wants to awaken us by saying, "You're building on sand! I can give you the stability you need, but you'll have to build according to My plan—not yours."

Haggai continued, "You hoped for rich harvests, but they were poor. And when you brought your harvest home, I blew it away. Why? Because My house lies in ruins, says the Lord of Heaven's armies, while all of you are busy building your own fine houses."[52]

The only Kingdom God is interested in building is the one that will last forever—His own. We can join Him in the marvelous task, but in any kingdom, only the king has a vote. The eternal Kingdom of God is no different. If we build on His eternal principles of trust and obedience, then God promises to bless our lives.

"Then…the whole remnant of God's people began to obey the message from the Lord their God. When they heard the words of the prophet Haggai, whom the Lord their God had sent, the people feared the Lord. Then Haggai, the Lord's messenger,

---

51 Haggai 1:5–8

52 Haggai 1:9

gave the people this message from the Lord: 'I am with you, says the Lord!'"[53]

In the next chapter, the prophet proclaims, "For this is what the Lord of Heaven's Armies says: In just a little while I will again shake the heavens and the earth, the oceans and the dry land. I will shake all the nations, and the treasures of all the nations will be brought to this Temple. I will fill this place with glory, says the Lord of Heaven's Armies."[54]

If we respond to God's shaking and stirring then, when He shakes the whole Earth, it won't be a wake-up call for us. Instead it will be a confirmation of what we have graciously been allowed to anticipate, having been divinely prepared by His Spirit and therefore ready to face all that is ahead.

God is eager to guide us in His perfect plan that will not fail.

THE GOD-CENTERED CHURCH

Paul the Apostle summed up so clearly the challenge set before us in his letter to the Corinthian church: "Anyone who builds on that foundation may use a variety of materials—gold, silver, jewels, wood, hay, or straw. But on the judgment day, fire will reveal what kind of work each builder has done. The fire will show if a person's work has any value. If the work survives, that builder will receive a reward. But if the work is burned up, the builder will suffer great loss. The builder will be saved, but like someone barely escaping through a wall of flames."[55]

May we each build wisely in anticipation of the storms ahead!

---

[53] Haggai 1:12–13

[54] Haggai 2:6–7

[55] 1Corinthians 3:12–15

In 2 Kings, the Aramean army laid siege on Jerusalem, not allowing food or drink into the city for many months. The people were desperate. "Now there were four men with leprosy sitting at the entrance of the city gates. 'Why should we sit here waiting to die?' they asked each other."[56] Being lepers, they were not welcome in the city. They therefore counted their lives as nothing and had nothing to lose.

They said to one another, "'We will starve if we stay here, but with the famine in the city, we will starve if we go back there. So we might as well go out and surrender to the Aramean army. If they let us live, so much the better. But if they kill us, we would have died anyway.' So at twilight they set out for the camp of the Arameans. But when they came to the edge of the camp, no one was there! For the Lord had caused the Aramean army to hear the clatter of speeding chariots and the galloping of horses and the sounds of a great army approaching. 'The king of Israel has hired the Hittites and Egyptians to attack us!' they cried to one another. So they panicked and ran into the night, abandoning their tents, horses, donkeys, and everything else, as they fled for their lives. When the lepers arrived at the edge of the camp, they went into one tent after another, eating and drinking wine; and they carried off silver and gold and clothing and hid it. Finally, they said to each other, 'This is not right. This is a day of good news, and we aren't sharing it with anyone! If we wait until morning, some calamity will certainly fall upon us. Come on, let's go back and tell the people at the palace.'"[57]

Like these blessed lepers, if we consider our lives as nothing unless we obey the Lord, we will then be able to bring life to those around us. We must be willing to humble ourselves before our Holy God and put on the spiritual sackcloth that demonstrates our desperate need of Him. If we allow ourselves to

---

[56] 2Kings 7:3

[57] 2Kings 7:4–9

be irritated to the point of action by the gross misrepresentation of Jesus, then we will at last demonstrate that Jesus truly lives in us.

We don't need to change our geographic location in order to accomplish this victory over evil. We simply need to allow God to change our perceptions of life.

We must lay ourselves on the altar. We must offer our bodies as living sacrifices. We must burn our idols and man-made cultural ideologies. We must die to self.

"I myself no longer live, but Christ lives in me. So I live my life in this earthly body by trusting in the Son of God, who loved me and gave Himself for me."[58]

After death and three days in the ground, the shaking begins, and resurrection springs up from the ground.

On the other side of our death is the Living Church of God's dreams.

Her Purpose is to be *Authentic*
Her Heart is to be *Accepting*
Her Destiny is to be *Transparent*
Her Focus is to be *Discerning*
Her Vision is to be *Supernatural*
Her Voice is to be *Virtual*
Though the Battle will increase when she is *Persecuted*,
Her Future is *Eternal* and cannot be taken away.

You are that Church.

And this is your story.

---

[58] Galatians 2:20

QUESTIONS FOR DISCUSSION

1. Are you fully committed to Jesus Christ as your Lord and Savior? How is this choice affecting your life and the lives around you?

2. How have you lost or gained ground since you first committed your life to Him? What impact has this had on your life and your relationships?

3. What initial steps do you need to take in order for your spiritual life to be growing and healthier?

4. What personal areas of compromise are most hindering you from fulfilling God's will for your life? How is that affecting you and others around you?

5. Do you believe your relationship with God's Word, worship, prayer, the local church, and with other believers is where it should be? What steps are you willing to take to improve any of these dimensions of your life?

AUTHENTIC CHURCH

CHAPTER TWO

"If you don't live it, it won't come out of your horn."
CHARLIE PARKER[1]

At 15 years old, I set the record straight between God and me. On a lonely walk, I told Him, "God, if you exist and you are like any of the people I know who claim to represent you, then we have nothing in common."

It would be seven years of periodic highs but far more frequent lows before I would crash-land as a suicidal, embittered atheist. Growing up with an authoritarian dad and living at a sterile Catholic boarding school had done its damage. Religion suffocated any desire for a relationship with God.

I was not the only one.

Today there are millions of spiritual refugees fleeing from the menagerie of churches and religions encircling the globe. Many of these now deeply wounded and un-whole individuals stand jeering on the sidelines, fully enraged over the abuse, hypocrisy, and outright misrepresentation of those who claimed to have a relationship with God.

Too many individuals asserting to be born again followers of Jesus have failed to live honest and sincere lives consistent

---

[1] Jazz saxophonist

> **Lack of authenticity is the biggest stumbling block facing Christians today.**

with the Word of God. Instead of being spiritual stepping-stones they have sadly become mere stumbling blocks to others.

The secular masses have not been oblivious to this lack of integrity. The hypocrisy demonstrated by pretend Christianity is obvious. The double-minded lives of professing Christians have been the elephant in the room for quite some time. Lack of authenticity is the biggest stumbling block facing Christians today.

Authentic has been defined as, "conforming to fact and therefore worthy of trust, reliance, or belief."[2] Is our relationship with Jesus so real, so authentically factual, that those around us want to trust, rely on and believe in the God we follow?

This is the question of the age.

In the first century Peter warned of those who would not take God's Holy Word seriously. He said they would twist and torture the truth to their own destruction. Every age has had them, and there is no shortage today. Peter wrote that these "untaught and unstable people twist [torture or pervert] to their own destruction, as they do also the rest of the Scriptures."[3]

The misrepresentation of God's heart and recorded Word by Christians continues to be the greatest distraction and hindrance to people finding Jesus, especially in the post-Christian Western world.

Jesus' original intent was that His followers would surrender to the transforming Word of God. If not, they could never be taken seriously and would eventually be lumped together with false religions and cults. Now, at the climax of the age, more people believe in the supernatural yet believe less in God.

---

2 *The American Heritage (R) Dictionary of the English Language, Fourth Edition* (Houghton Mifflin Company, 2004).

3 2Peter 3:16a, NKJV

What is heaven's answer to this greatest of all anomalies?

It is the resurrection of the genuine Christian. The real disciples of Jesus Christ will rise to reclaim their stewardship as salt and light on the Earth.

In the days of Jesus, He passionately drove out gross misrepresentation of God from the temple in Jerusalem.[4] Once again, the Spirit of God is rising to drive all disingenuousness out of His Church.

Likewise, prior to the first coming of Jesus, John the Baptist challenged the religious leaders of his day to, "Prove by the way you live that you have repented of your sins and turned to God. Even now the ax of God's judgment is poised, ready to sever the roots of the trees. Yes, every tree that does not produce good fruit will be chopped down and thrown into the fire."[5]

Today, anyone desiring an authentic relationship with God should be able to meet Christians who are sincere, open, transparent, loving and caring representatives of Jesus Christ— especially if they're coming to church.

This is what Christ always intended, and it will come to pass prior to His return. It is our dying to self and living for God that will help heal those who were once wounded and are longing to see a pure demonstration of the legitimate life of God in the Spirit.

In this book, I am crying out to you who hear His call to rise up and receive the destiny preserved for those who live desperate to know God. We are called to be an honest expression of His genuine life. We are birthed in reality, sustained in humility, and destined to bring glory to His flawless name.

Once again, the Spirit of God is rising to drive all disingenuousness out of His Church.

---

[4] Matthew 21:12, Mark 11:15

[5] Matthew 3:8,10

PURE REJECTION

"And all of us have had that veil removed so that we can be mirrors that brightly reflect the glory of the Lord. And as the Spirit of the Lord works within us, we become more and more like Him and reflect His glory even more."

2 CORINTHIANS 3:18

In the next and most challenging season of all time, Christ's followers will be faced with an important question: Will this generation fully reflect the glory of God?

> **Each day the world groans in agony, having suffered senseless wounds at the hands of those who distort His image.**

God has given every person on Earth a deep, inner longing to experience and express His true heart—to live from the inside out. This alone will genuinely represent Him and turn the world upside down.[6] Will we rise to claim our true identity and inheritance as sons and daughters of the Creator of the universe, or will we settle for being cultural clones, moral zombies, and counterfeits of all that He created us to be?

It is my conviction that many of us who claim intimacy with God have seen enough of His heart to reflect Him. After all, we have been rescued from death, salvaged from destruction and fully redeemed!

Yet, each day the world groans in agony, having suffered senseless wounds at the hands of those who distort God's image.

The danger of this level of deception was evident from the beginning of creation and will always lead to perhaps the greatest of all evils—knowingly misrepresenting God. This may be the sin that most damages the trusting human heart and

---

[6] Acts 17:6

brings the severest punishment. Scripture, as we will examine later in this chapter, strongly implies this.

Because he rejected the outstretched arms of God, Lucifer was cast down from Heaven. Having been created to bask in the splendor of God's radiant presence and reflect His transcendent beauty, the "son of the morning" chose instead to exalt himself above God. This senior worship leader of Heaven openly resisted God's love, inflicting an endless wound upon his formerly blessed life and becoming the most tragic misrepresentation of all that is good.

He had seen so much but understood so little.

Later on Earth, a similar misdeed took place. Judas, one of the original twelve apostles, spent years witnessing firsthand the kindness of God through the life of Jesus. He, too, foolishly chose to live a lie and betrayed the Son of man with a kiss. Of him, Jesus lamented, "It would be far better for that man if he had never been born."[7]

Like Lucifer, Judas was given so much and appreciated so little.

In a comparable way, two of the first disciples mentioned in the Book of Acts, Ananias and Sapphira, vainly attempted to deceive the Holy Spirit. They fell over dead for such blatant deceit.[8]

They, too, had seen so much and yet learned so little.

For each of these attempts to deceive the Father, Son and Holy Spirit, these once-favored creations of God received swift and final repercussions. Any fully informed and honest court on Earth would have issued the same verdict. It is painfully obvious that they knew better. Even today, the damage of dishonesty and duplicity can be life-long. In a world of imitations, there is no substitute for the genuine.

---

[7] Matthew 26:24

[8] Acts 5:1–11

Either we who claim to know the truth must live lives that authentically represent the God who is Truth, or we will inadvertently become co-conspirators with the father of lies himself.[9] Should our own misrepresentation of the truth make us any less culpable than Satan? Jesus emphasized the opposite as true when He said, "But someone who does not know, and then does something wrong, will be punished only lightly. When someone has been given much, much will be required in return; and when someone has been entrusted with much, even more will be required."[10]

The long-term dangers of misrepresentation become even more alarming upon closer examination.

On a few occasions, the disciples of Jesus openly asked which of them would be the greatest in Heaven. This gave Jesus a perfect opportunity to not only correct the twisted motive behind their misguided question, but also to sum up the grave consequences of intentionally stumbling one of His innocent children. Without mincing words Jesus warned His followers of the severe punishment awaiting those who wound vulnerable yet sincere followers of Jesus: "But if you cause one of these little ones who trusts in me to fall into sin, it would be better for you to have a large millstone tied around your neck and be drowned in the depths of the sea."[11]

In my own youth, it was the misrepresentation of God that caused me to hate Him and spend seven empty years as an adamant atheist. But a single, authentic encounter with Jesus saved me. My life was transformed when I saw Jesus genuinely reflected in a person I trusted.

While on Earth, Jesus Christ was the perfect representation of the character and heart of God. After Jesus' ascent into Heaven, the Holy Spirit was then sent to inhabit the spirit of each sincere follower of Christ. This strategic plan was designed to

---

9 John 8:44

10 Luke 12:48

11 Matthew 18:6

secure an authentic incarnation of God's goodness and kindness on Earth. God's original strategy is still best: "For we are the temple of the living God. As God said: 'I will live in them and walk among them. I will be their God, and they will be My people.'"[12]

Before the final harvest and the end of the age, there will be a pure representation of God's intended church.

I am completely convinced that before the final harvest and the end of the age, there will be a pure representation of God's intended church. God's Word will not return without accomplishing His original purpose.[13]

"For God wanted them to know that the riches and glory of Christ are for you Gentiles, too. And this is the secret: Christ lives in you. This gives you assurance of sharing His glory."[14]

HOPE SPRINGS

An empty heart is the damaged fruit of hopelessness. Half-heartedness is the distracted fruit of deception. Whole-heartedness is the enlightened fruit of a heart fully embracing the grace of God.

This whole-hearted acceptance of God's grace is the backbone of authenticity. "Partially authentic" is an oxymoron. Authenticity and integrity go hand-in-hand. Together they release a spiritual endorphin, providing a deep sense of inner wellbeing.

So why are single-minded, whole-hearted, authentic Christians hard to find?

Winner of the Nobel Peace Prize Elie Wiesel writes, "Only one enemy is worse than despair: indifference. In every area of human creativity, indifference is the enemy; indifference of evil is worse than evil, because it is also sterile."

---

12 2Corinthians 6:16, Jeremiah 24:7, Ezekiel 37:27

13 Isaiah 55:11

14 Colossians 1:27

He should know. He was a Holocaust survivor.

Half-heartedness can only creep in due to some level of indifference.[15] And while the half-hearted are trapped in indifference, the empty-hearted are searching long and hard for any vestige of genuine hope on Earth.

They find many counterfeits. Imposters on Earth offer the false hope of their political, social, or even spiritual agendas. A closer examination of man-made hope reveals mere wishful thinking—a dreamscape of humans playing God. It always ends badly. From the Tower of Babel to the Titanic, facing the unexpected without the God of Hope leads to hopelessness.

Many would say that false hope has never been more plentiful, but I am convinced that the genuine article is closer than we think, once we know how to get it.

Years ago when I was globetrotting the world, racking up millions of miles on many an airline, I noticed that almost every restaurant carried Tabasco sauce. One day, upon taking a closer look at the tiny bottle, I read that Tabasco sauce was produced and bottled in one place: an island made of salt—Avery Island, Louisiana. One hundred and forty miles north of New Orleans, swamps and marshes surround the pepper fields of Avery Island. Since the first time I read the fine print on its tiny red bottle over a quarter of a century ago, I have picked up many additional bottles of Tabasco, knowing that the original still comes from just one place.

So too with eternal hope!

While the poet wrote with flowery speech and all sincerity, "Hope springs eternal in the human breast,"[16] never forget that genuine hope is produced and dispersed from only one source: the river of life, flowing from the throne of God in

---

15 Matthew 22:5

16 Alexander Pope, English poet from the eighteenth century

Heaven. Hope springs from one source alone: God.[17] Unless it is bottled in Heaven, earthly hope eventually dries up.

So where can the empty-hearted find hope? It is from God alone that we receive and then freely give the hopeless masses the elixir of life: Heavenly hope. The Authentic Church carries the answer to a hopeless world. Christ in YOU is the hope of glory![18]

Without personally receiving our daily dose of the hope that refuses to disappoint,[19] we will inevitably lose the wind of assurance in our sails. The result will be, for a season, that we will continue to live the charade of believing we still retain God's priceless gift of life, even though its true value has long since evaporated. Or, worse yet, we will give up—wallowing in the depressed caverns of discouragement, unable to rescue even ourselves.

Only God and those who trust in Him have the right to be eternal optimists. The rest of the planet will scavenge for hope until at last they realize God owns the rights to all of the hope that has ever existed. It is being freely offered but on God's terms. Heavenly hope in the hands of the earthly minded will lose its lift, having been detached from its source.

I have been empty-hearted without God, half-hearted due to a lapse of relationship with God, and thankfully, now for many years, whole-hearted, drinking from the artesian well of Heavenly hope continually emanating from the God of hope.

Draw close to the well and open your heart.

There's plenty of hope for everyone.

---

17 Revelation 22:1

18 Colossians 1:27

19 Romans 5:5

STARVED SURRENDER

The literary genius Victor Hugo once wrote, "An invasion of armies can be resisted, but not an idea whose time has come."

The time has come for each of us to make a massive move toward absolute surrender to the will of God.

In 2 Kings 6, it was also the time to surrender.

A king named Ben-Hadad surrounded and attacked the city of Samaria. The siege was intended to prevent all intra-business and trade in order to eventually starve the population into surrender.

"As a result," the Bible says, "there was a great famine in the city. The siege lasted so long that a donkey's head sold for eighty pieces of silver [a year's wages], and a cup of dove's dung sold for five pieces of silver [a month's wages]."[20] These people were so starved for real food that they spent inordinate amounts of money for imitation food.

When Hannibal besieged Casiline, France, in 200 B.C., a mouse was sold for the equivalent of $4. These events parallel our present-day culture and even what is taking place within the Church in the Western world. In this age of moral compromise, we see a culture that is increasingly overreacting, under-reacting, or just plain "acting," as it is surrounded and besieged by unprecedented evil.

Both the world and the Church are equally starving for the genuine article: real humility, real authority, real integrity, real honesty, and real love and compassion—in short, the real presence of God.

---

[20] 2Kings 6:25

Frankly, this is what is missing in everyone's life. It's priceless. We're so hungry for these authentic dimensions of life that we unknowingly pay exorbitant amounts for false love and intimacy.

> **We unknowingly pay exorbitant amounts for false love and intimacy.**

The story in 2 Kings continues: "One day as the king of Israel was walking along the wall of the city, a woman called to him, 'Please help me, my lord the king!' He answered, 'If the LORD doesn't help you, what can I do? I have neither food from the threshing floor nor wine from the press to give you.' But then the king asked, 'What is the matter?' She replied, 'This woman said to me: "Come on, let's eat your son today, then we will eat my son tomorrow." So we cooked my son and ate him. Then the next day I said to her, "Kill your son so we can eat him," but she has hidden her son.' When the king heard this, he tore his clothes in despair. And as the king walked along the wall, the people could see that he was wearing burlap under his robe next to his skin."[21]

It may seem hard to believe that this event could have actually happened. But living in today's unthinkable age, we can easily see how once the spiritual, moral and ethical foundations within a society are destroyed, all levels of depravity are fair game.

Anarchy has been defined as "a state of disorder due to absence or non-recognition of authority."[22] It is derived from the Greek word anarkhos, meaning "without a chief ruler." Once we choose to remove ourselves from the protective covering of a loving and faithful Creator, we are plunged into the abyss of relativism, uncertainty and compromise. As the psalmist once wrote, "If the foundations are destroyed, what can the righteous do?"[23]

---

[21] 2Kings 6:26–30

[22] *The New Oxford American Dictionary* (Oxford University Press, 2001).

[23] Psalm 11:3, NKJV

Either we return to the foundation of being under the rulership of our Creator, or we eventually compromise every dimension of our lives.

One of the saddest seductions of all is the obsession to look for the solution to life's dilemmas in the heart of man. From capitalists to communists, socialists to secularists, no political or economic system can keep self-indulgence and hypocrisy from raising their ugly heads. Excess and deceit are lodged in the human heart. Man playing God only makes it worse.

When people grow weary of the greed of unscrupulous capitalists, they naively accept the thievery of socialists. The former system tends to seduce those who have to get even more, at times making little provision for the less fortunate. The later structure penalizes the diligent, rewarding the indolent. Either path is a ticking time bomb if the inner man is not transformed. The Bible clearly asserts it is the "heart that is deceitful above all things."[24] Only a commitment to follow the heart of God can bring the compassion and community that are essential to create the society God intended, and man longs for.

---

[24] Jeremiah 17:9

BORING YOURSELF TO DEATH

German philosopher and renowned atheist, Friedrich Nietzsche, candidly admitted his tedious life experience when he penned, "Against boredom the gods themselves fight in vain."[25] Tragically, Nietzsche did not link his self-inflicted dullness to a lack of connection with his Creator.

Spiritual boredom is the root of many sins.

It rejects reality for fantasy and forsakes illumination for illusion.

Only the Creator of all things establishes reality. Nothing has substance or value outside of His divine intention. Though man-made creations appear to have meaning in this momentary, transitory world, they have no lasting consequence.

When Lucifer refused to embrace the reality of his exalted yet subservient position before an all-powerful God, he was thrust out of God's eternal reality into a self-inflicted exile from all that he truly longed for.

Likewise, Adam and Eve left fact for fiction, ceasing to fight for what was true and authentic in the Garden of Eden. They allowed their marvelous imaginations to become intoxicated by the promise of an imposter. The corrupting allure of something beyond what the perfect God had so graciously provided for them jettisoned the chosen first couple outside the reach of the Tree of Life, where they forsook their eternal destiny. Deluded and dismayed, they lost touch with their Father.

An angelic sentry was placed at the entrance of the Garden to prevent their return. "After sending them out, the LORD God stationed mighty cherubim to the east of the Garden of Eden. And He placed a flaming sword that flashed back and forth to guard the way to the tree of life."[26]

---

25 Nietzsche F. *The Anti-Christ* (1895).

26 Genesis 3:24

> **Having forsaken the spontaneous adventure of walking hand-in-hand with their Maker, they vainly attempt becoming gods of their own lives.**

God will not let reality be contaminated by delusion. He will protect and preserve His perfect plan. Only submitting to the God of reality will allow our reentry into the original relational bliss He intended. Anything less than intimacy with our Creator will consign us to aimless toil day after day, conjuring up alternate endings to our lives that will frankly never come to pass.

This is why so many Christians today are bored to death plodding through their predictable lives. Having forsaken the spontaneous adventure of walking hand-in-hand with their Maker, they vainly attempt becoming gods of their own lives.

Do they settle for a make-believe god because they have never experienced the exhilarating relationship of actually knowing Him, or have they ceased to pursue the One who alone can fulfill their deepest longings?

Being genuine has always required a whole-hearted commitment, a passionate focus on peeling back layers of repetitive behavior for a fresh experience in God. Compared to knowing the living God, the cruel drudgery of this world is but a painful hallucination, a throwback to an ancient rebellion that has long-since failed.

MISFIRE

I will have greater impact on people when I humbly admit I'm wrong than when I'm consistently right. We can only meet the God of forgiveness when we admit we have sinned against Him. Since knowing God is a universal need, this is the primary relationship people want to see working in us. Yet owning our mistakes is often one of the most difficult things for us to do.

Until I can freely admit I have been wrong, I am firing blanks in my Christian life.

A man named John Corcoran never learned to read or write in grade school and had to hide it from everyone when he got to high school. "I started cheating by turning in other peoples' papers," he confessed. "(I) dated the valedictorian and ran around with college prep kids. I couldn't read words but I could read the system and I could read people."[27]

Upon graduating, John got an athletic scholarship to Texas Western College. He cheated his way to a diploma and, ironically, received a degree in education. Even more astounding is the fact that he was hired as a teacher. For 17 years, John taught in high school, and yet he had no ability to read or write. He recounts, "What I did was I created an oral and visual environment. There wasn't the written word in there. I always had two or three teacher's assistants in each class to do board work or read the bulletin."

After a career in education, he became a real estate developer. Only much later in life did he acknowledge the lie he had been living and finally learn to read and write. Not surprisingly he became a spokesperson for improving our educational system.

How many Christians go through the motions of Christianity, parroting what they believe, but not living it? The great British preacher Charles Haddon Spurgeon said, "When you see a

---

[27] Yu C. Retired Teacher Reveals He Was Illiterate Until Age 48. Channel 10 News. February 11, 2008. Available at http://www.10news.com/news/15274005/detail.html. Last accessed July 15, 2009.

great deal of religion displayed in his shop window, you may depend on it, that he keeps a very small stock of it within."

Is there consistency between what we say and who we are?

Do our parents, spouse and children see the same person our church friends and co-workers see?

Are we bored to death, suffering from a lack of actual spiritual life?

It seems empty talk is more prevalent in the church than we would care to admit. But we all strain to see actual life, honest humility and someone who is really walking the talk.

At the 1924 Paris Olympics, Eric Liddell was the fastest man alive. The Scotsman won a gold medal, but victory wasn't the high point of Eric's life. His ultimate destiny was to go to China as a missionary. He eventually died while in a Japanese Concentration Camp during two years of internment in World War II. Eric Liddell emerged as its "…most outstanding personality. The one with a permanent smile."[28] One Russian prostitute said he was "the only man who did anything for her without wanting to be repaid."[29]

Can patterns of ineffectiveness be changed? Absolutely!

Focused attention to transform what seems to have little value can lead to the creation of that which is priceless. If you don't believe me, ask U.S. automakers if the identification "Made in Japan" still makes them laugh.

---

[28] Myers DG, Jeeves MA. *Psychology Through the Eyes of Faith* (HarperCollins, 1987:207).

[29] Ibid.

THE CURSE OF COMPROMISE

Noah Webster defined hypocrisy as "a simulation; a feigning to be what one is not; a concealment of one's real character or motives. More generally, hypocrisy is the assuming of a false appearance of virtue or religion; a deceitful show of a good character, in morals or religion; a counterfeiting of religion."[30]

What a striking definition! How profoundly clearly this man, known as the "Father of American Scholarship and Education," recognized hypocrisy. It is a simulation, a fake, a sham, concealing the real person. In particular it refers to someone who professes a spiritual conviction but lives a double life.

Originally, hypocrisy was derived from the Greek word *hypokrisis,* which meant, "play acting."[31] It was a theatrical term used in ancient Greece to describe those acting out.

Centuries later, hypocrisy is the one sin Jesus most aggressively exposed. He repeatedly rebuked the Scribes and Pharisees of His day, chastising them for their duplicity. Frankly, it puts the fear of God in me to read the many verses in the Gospels where Jesus refers to the religious leaders of His day as phonies.

"What sorrow awaits you teachers of religious law and you Pharisees. Hypocrites! For you shut the door of the Kingdom of Heaven in people's faces. You won't go in yourselves, and you don't let others enter either."[32]

To think that my actions, or lack thereof, could literally keep someone from spending eternity in Heaven shakes me to my core. My responsibility to authentically represent the Lord has eternal consequences; both for my own life and for those I have been called to shepherd. This is why Christian leaders

---

30 Noah Webster's 1828 American Dictionary

31 *Pocket Oxford Classical Greek Dictionary.* Ed Morwood, Taylor (Oxford University Press, 2002).

32 Matthew 23:13

> **This modern age is littered with once-gallant vessels who fell prey to compromise.**

and teachers will receive a much greater judgment for their words and deeds than will their followers.

James, the brother of Jesus, candidly wrote, "Dear brothers and sisters, not many of you should become teachers in the church, for we who teach will be judged more strictly."[33] It is God alone who will judge what is in the heart of man.[34] John Milton wisely mused, "For neither man nor angel can discern hypocrisy, the only evil that walks invisible, except to God alone."[35]

This modern age is littered with once-gallant vessels who fell prey to compromise, losing their ministries and even families in exchange for that which would not satisfy. Pastor Charles Swindoll writes of the effects of this deception, "The swift wind of compromise is a lot more devastating than the sudden jolt of misfortune."[36]

Somehow the misfortunes and adversities that each of us endure leave no blemish on our character or integrity. Compromise, on the other hand, can unravel the trust and respect attained over an entire lifetime. As the psalmist wrote in desperation, "Keep your servant from deliberate sins! Don't let them control me. Then I will be free of guilt and innocent of great sin."[37]

---

[33] James 3:1

[34] Romans 2:16

[35] Milton J. *Paradise Lost* (England, 1667).

[36] Swindoll CR. *Autumn-A Season of Reflection: Growing Strong in the Seasons of Life* (Zondervan, 1994:387).

[37] Psalm 19:13

THE "JESUS-LITE" BACKLASH

Living less than Jesus intended always brings a backlash. It will eventually lead to disgrace and regret.

When Barry Bonds hit his 756th home run, breaking Hank Aaron's longstanding record, his veracity was called into question by allegations that he used performance-enhancing steroids to accomplish the feat. Many sports enthusiasts thought there should be an asterisk next to his name in the record books footnoting that the record was in some way tainted.

As the idea was tossed around, the highly successful entrepreneur who bought the famed ball asked baseball fans in an Internet poll what he should do with the record-setting baseball. The poll indicated that the fans wanted the ball branded with an asterisk and donated to the baseball Hall of fame—and that's exactly what he did.

Throughout the ages, some of Christ's followers have cut corners and lowered the bar of commitment to Jesus. This "easy-believism," or "Jesus-lite," as it's sometimes called, diminishes the level of transformation in their own lives, leading to a gradual distortion of the way, the truth, and the life God intended us to live. In time, it always brings a reproach and taints the impact our lives can have as true representatives of Jesus Christ. Jesus gave us an irrefutable equation, "What you say flows from what is in your heart."[38]

Perhaps, there are even eternal repercussions. The last book in the Bible emphatically states that in the Final Judgment, "Nothing evil will be allowed to enter, nor anyone who practices shameful idolatry and dishonesty—but only those whose names are written in the Lamb's Book of Life."[39]

---

[38] Luke 6:45b
[39] Revelation 21:27

On the other hand, Jesus promised, "All who are victorious will be clothed in white. I will never erase their names from the Book of Life, but I will announce before My Father and His angels that they are mine."[40]

Paul the martyred Apostle also wrote, "And having chosen them, He called them to come to Him. And having called them, He gave them right standing with Himself. And having given them right standing, He gave them His glory."[41]

May there be no asterisk next to our names in the Lamb's Book of Life. May we finish well as Paul did when he wrote, "I have fought the good fight, I have finished the race, and I have remained faithful. And now the prize awaits me—the crown of righteousness, which the Lord, the righteous Judge, will give me on the day of His return. And the prize is not just for me but for all who eagerly look forward to His appearing."[42]

THE SPIRIT OF CYNICISM

We live in the age of cynics. Sarcasm is king and mockery his queen.

Someone once defined, "A cynic is a man who, when he smells flowers, looks around for a coffin."[43] For the cynic, nothing is sacred, and all things foul are fair game.

The plague of taunting and teasing begins as early as possible and has become almost a rite of passage within the youth culture. No one escapes its debasing effects. Everyone is deflated in order to elevate the cynic.

---

40 Revelation 3:5

41 Romans 8:30

42 2Timothy 4:7-8

43 H. L. Mencken, American Editor, Author, Critic, Humorist, 1880–1956.

A preacher once said, "The cynic is one who never sees a good quality in a man, and never fails to see a bad one. He is the human owl, vigilant in darkness and blind to light."[44]

Because cynics inherently believe the worst about other people, they've been described as those "who believe that everyone is motivated primarily by self-interest rather than by acting honorably or for unselfish reasons."[45]

Jesus warned us to not allow a critical spirit to overtake our lives when He said, "And why worry about a speck in your friend's eye when you have a log in your own?"[46] If I want to be critical of someone, let me start with myself. But even then, John the beloved disciple wrote, "For if our heart condemns us, God is greater than our heart, and knows all things."[47]

It's pretty clear from scripture that Lucifer, the rebellious archangel, is the father of all cynics. He duped and probably ridiculed one-third of the angels in heaven to buy into his doomed coup[48] and now he spends his time surfing the globe, ridiculing as many unfortunate victims as possible.

The word ridicule is derived from the Latin *ridiculum*, where we also get the word ridiculous, meaning "laughable." Jesus rebuked the ridiculing leaders of His day, saying that this negativity identified their true father and misrepresented His. "For you are the children of your father the devil, and you love to do the evil things he does. He was a murderer from the beginning. He has always hated the truth, because there is no truth in him. When he lies, it is consistent with his character, for he is a liar and the father of lies. So when I tell the truth, you just naturally don't believe me!"[49]

---

[44] Henry Ward Beecher, American Preacher, Orator, Writer, 1813–1887.

[45] "Cynic." The Oxford Pocket Dictionary of Current English. 2009. Encyclopedia.com 23 Apr. 2009 http://www.encyclopedia.com

[46] Matthew 7:3

[47] 1John 3:20, NKJV

[48] Revelation 12:4, 9

[49] John 8:44–45

The infection of condescending, belittling, derogatory humor within all aspects of contemporary culture is epidemic. Talk shows, sit-coms, blogs, comedians, pundits, and every venue of social networking provide a daily barrage of deprecating and destructive hate-speech, which, like cursing, devalues the God-given dignity of both those who say it and hear it.

The infection of condescending, belittling, derogatory humor within all aspects of contemporary culture is epidemic.

This avalanche of negative communication destroys marriages, families, friendships, and even churches. Cynicism is a cancer polluting the planet. It was birthed in hell, so to hell it will one day return. Until that liberating day, we must be vigilant to "Live wisely among those who are not believers, and make the most of every opportunity. Let your conversation be gracious and attractive so that you will have the right response for everyone."[50]

As Paul, the once embittered Pharisee, so eloquently articulated near the end of his well-lived life, "And now, dear brothers and sisters, one final thing. Fix your thoughts on what is true, and honorable, and right, and pure, and lovely, and admirable. Think about things that are excellent and worthy of praise."[51]

God intends for authentic followers of Jesus to rise, becoming a pure, lovely and admirable Authentic Church!

---

[50] Colossians 4:5–6

[51] Philippians 4:8

QUESTIONS FOR DISCUSSION

1. Have you been hurt by other Christians who have not represented Jesus in an authentic and healthy way? In what ways did that experience affect you?

2. Have you personally misrepresented Jesus in a way that you know has hurt another person's Christian faith? How did your misrepresentation affect that person?

3. What dimensions of authenticity are most important to you? (E.g. integrity, honesty, humility, genuineness, etc.) Why?

4. Are there areas in your life that need to be transformed in order for you to represent Jesus in an authentic way? What are they and what is your next step?

5. Are there people you need to ask to forgive you for misrepresenting Jesus? If so, write out their names and a plan for going to them and asking for forgiveness (in person, a letter, a phone call).

3 ACCEPTING CHURCH

CHAPTER THREE

"The good neighbor looks beyond the external accidents and discerns those inner qualities that make all men human and, therefore, brothers."

REV. MARTIN LUTHER KING JR.[1]

A Jewish man was beaten, robbed by thieves and left severely wounded on the side of the road. A priest and temple assistant walked by and did nothing. But, most surprisingly, a despised Samaritan gathered him up, took him to an inn, and paid for the stranger's recovery.

Jesus compassionately told this Parable when an expert in religious law asked, "Who is my neighbor?"[2] After recounting this allegory, Jesus asked, "Now which of these three would you say was a neighbor to the man who was attacked by bandits?" The religious expert replied, "The one who showed him mercy." Then Jesus said, "Yes, now go and do the same."[3]

This command to genuinely love our neighbor has never been rescinded. It remains today as a directive from the God of compassion to all of His true followers on Earth.

---

1 King Jr ML. *Strength to Love* (Harper & Row, 1963).

2 Luke 10:25–37

3 Luke 10:36–37

Whole-heartedly accepting and loving all people, no matter who they are, what they believe, or what they have done, is not giving in to coercion or intimidation. Godly acceptance is not a forced reaction out of fear; it is a chosen response out of love. "Love has no fear because perfect love expels all fear."[4]

As Paul wrote, "For the love of Christ compels us…"[5] and, "Owe nothing to anyone—except for your obligation to love one another. If you love your neighbor, you will fulfill the requirements of God's law."[6]

The Church of tomorrow will redefine tolerance for a compromising generation. Instead of criticism, comparison and prejudice, she will love perfectly, accept willingly, and adopt wholeheartedly.

ACCEPTANCE WITHOUT COMPROMISE

In every age, the true followers of God have been presented with the intimidating option of giving in to the crowd. Be it before kings, oppressors, or peers, the temptation came. In the cases of Daniel, Shadrach, Meshach, Abednego, Esther and Stephen, each refused to give up eternal inheritance for momentary security.

When threatened with death for not worshipping an earthly king, "Shadrach, Meshach, and Abednego replied, 'O Nebuchadnezzar, we do not need to defend ourselves before you. If we are thrown into the blazing furnace, the God whom we serve is able to save us. He will rescue us from your power, Your Majesty. But even if He doesn't, we want to make it clear to you, Your Majesty, that we will never serve your gods or worship the gold statue you have set up.'"[7]

---

4 1John 4:18a

5 2Corinthians 5:14

6 Romans 13:8

7 Daniel 3:16–18

Fear of man is perhaps the greatest temptation lying in wait for the End Time Church. It is a trap that invariably leads to compromise of convictions and jettisons deceived hearts outside of God's will and protection.

We must never yield in fear to those around us. Instead, we should yield to God in joyful obedience. As the Apostle John so emphatically wrote, "But you belong to God, my dear children. You have already won a victory over those people, because the Spirit who lives in you is greater than the spirit who lives in the world."[8]

> **A merely "tolerant" heart will lead to picking and choosing which neighbor is worthy of our acceptance, love and care.**

Does this scripture resonate in your spirit? Personally, it stirs me to act on my conviction.

I will not bow timidly to man!

I will yield in humility to God!

I will turn my cheek and run the extra mile for my brother, not because of cowardice, but because I've received the courage God gives to all who bow to Him alone. I believe with all of my heart that "My victory and honor come from God alone. He is my refuge, a rock where no enemy can reach me."[9]

A merely "tolerant" heart will lead to picking and choosing which neighbor is worthy of our acceptance, love and care. A heart yielded to the God of love realizes it is not our decision to make, but God's command to obey.

---

[8] 1John 4:4

[9] Psalm 62:7

TRUE TOLERANCE

Tolerance is defined as, "the ability or willingness to tolerate something. In particular, the existence of opinions or behavior that one does not necessarily agree with."[10]

This definition states that in order to be considered tolerant, we must be willing to put up with something we don't agree with. It doesn't say we have to agree with, speak well of, or embrace differing opinions.

If the latter is what it takes to be tolerant, then NO, I don't want to be tolerant.

I will instead commit to be much, much more.

I will look into the eyes of those I disagree with on moral and spiritual issues and tell them I love them, even when I know that their beliefs and lifestyles are detrimental to their good and contrary to God's best. I will endeavor to not just put up with but also to love even those who vehemently disagree with me, and I with them.

This is how Jesus loves us.

I must do no less to others.

I don't want to be tolerant. I will instead commit to be much, much more.

Some will misunderstand my heart and actions, as in the case of the Samaritan woman at the well.[11] She was shocked that Jesus, being a Jew, would be so kind and gracious to someone most Israelites considered a half-breed. But this is the calling upon the lives of all true Christians—those who know the God of love are to share it freely.

---

10 Apple Dictionary, Version 2.0.2

11 John 4:9

Recently, my wife and I had lunch with a dear friend whom I have known since 1972. For decades he lived the gay lifestyle and, from his own confession, was reckless. He knows it is only by God's grace that he doesn't have AIDS or some other dreadful disease.

A few weeks prior to our lunch, one of his relatives told him he was "possessed by evil spirits," because of his same-sex attraction. After 40-years of dealing with this issue, this comment by an evangelical Christian left him so distraught he contemplated suicide. In this emotionally worn out state, he reached out to my wife and I for help, encouragement, and support.

We had the most enjoyable time together even though we don't agree on some very important areas. For example, my wife and I believe marriage was designed by God to be between a man and a woman. He knows what Suzie and I believe, and that we disagree with his interpretation of certain passages of Scripture.

But our love for him is unshakeable!

We care for him dearly, and that afternoon we had conveyed our hearts so fully and completely that he called us after the luncheon, crying. He gratefully expressed that we had not just had lunch with him, but that we had prepared a feast on the finest china, making him feel heard, valued and cared for.

My wife and I have been working on doing just that with one another, every day, for over 33 years. We disagree, sometimes daily, on many things. But there has never been a disagreement about our love for each other.

During our lunch, my friend began to share his journey with us. It was a heart-breaking story of a lifetime of unrelenting pain. He recounted how he was aware of being very "different" as early as eight or nine-years old, describing the verbal assaults and cruel taunts he received from classmates who called him "sissy, fairy, faggot, queer and pansy." Such name-calling is so damaging to a young child.

When my friend was eleven, being more aware than ever of his same-sex attraction, he asked a well-known evangelist to pray over him for "deliverance from the demons of homosexuality." After this prayer he waited and waited for some kind, any kind of healing. None came. He told us that by then he was fully consumed with self-loathing, guilt, shame, and condemnation.

At 17, in desperation to become straight, he walked into his local Mental Health Clinic to get electroshock therapy. This type of primitive and inhumane treatment was widely used in the 60's and 70's to literally shock people with very painful electrical voltage, attempting to "change their behavior."

Two years later, a well-meaning female church member told him, "Girls would be more attracted to you if you weren't so effeminate." He was so hurt by the comment he came very close to taking his life later that night.

At 24, he joined an "ex-gay ministry," and was part of this group for almost three years. Ironically, the ministry was predominantly filled with other young men who had been raised in evangelical homes.

One of the saddest things my friend shared during our five-hour meeting was that he was convinced all of the years of guilt and self-loathing pushed him into a shameful three-decade pattern of promiscuous behavior with other men. Having been told his whole life how terrible and evil he was, he began to think, "Well, if I'm as bad as they say I am, then I might as well act terrible and evil!"

As a pastor, in order to see a genuine healing in people, I've tried to uncover WHY people do what they do—the root, and not so much WHAT they do—the fruit. My friend felt he had been raised in an environment where he was never told he had value or that he was "fearfully and wonderfully made."[12]

---

12 Psalm 139:14

I'm happy to report that my friend is finally making choices in his life that are healthy. He shared that once he finally accepted who he was in God's eyes, and maintained a strong, intimate relationship with Jesus, the promiscuity TOTALLY STOPPED! He joyfully proclaims that he's never been at such peace with himself as he is at this point of his life, being confident and resting in the love of God.

> **One minute before I opened my life and invited Him in, I was in rebellion, but He was in love.**

Shouldn't this be the same kind of love we extend to those around us? Isn't this precisely how Jesus loves us?

He doesn't agree with everything we believe, say, and do, but He never wavers in His love and concern for us. He makes a distinction between who we are to Him and the foolish things we do. Even those sinful actions that distort our true identity and bring harm to our lives cannot separate us from His love.

Frankly, there's nothing we could ever do to make God love us more or less than He always does. He is constantly at peak love for each of us. He is not just a God of love, but also a God in love—in love with every one of His children, not just the ones who are endeavoring to whole-heartedly follow Him.

He loved me when I openly mocked Him and His Word, ridiculed sincere Christians, and even laughed at my saintly mother as she prayed over her food. I resisted His Spirit for years until I was bankrupt of all that He had intended for my life. Yet, God was loving me every painful moment.

One minute before I opened my life and invited Him in, I was in rebellion, but He was in love. One minute after I surrendered my life to Him, His love had not increased one degree.

How could it?

He was already loving me with all of His heart.

GOD DOESN'T TOLERATE US

I pastor a wayward spiritual daughter who is periodically caught up in the lesbian lifestyle, trying to find the fulfillment only her Creator can give her. I've spent years reaching into her precious life. On countless occasions I have cried out to God to rescue her from what cannot satisfy and will only deeply wound her. I believe if you were to ask her if she knows I love her, she would give an emphatic, "Yes!" On one occasion she told me I am the only "father" she has ever had.

But she was, for a long time, far from the One who has no interest in "tolerating" her choices. Nevertheless, He loves her more than we can begin to imagine, with a love that will never die, and desires to embrace her.[13]

I have no interest in tolerating her, but I am deeply committed to loving her.

In 2008, Proposition 8 was on the ballot in California to establish a constitutional amendment stating that marriage is only between a man and a woman. Another young lady, who is 17-years old, and whom I love very much, saw someone from our church carrying a yard sign supporting the amendment. She completely freaked out and, with confusion and anger etched across her face, blurted, "What's that doing here?"

I had spent a lot of time with her and a dozen other teenage girls in her group home, all of whom struggled with drugs and serious emotional challenges, many believing they were lesbians or bisexual. She had devoured my book, *Father Wounds*, having had a major breach with her own father.

Because she knew I genuinely loved and cared for her, I was able to reach out and embrace her at that fragile moment. "Even though you don't understand right now, God has created marriage as a holy covenant between a man and a woman."

---

[13] Jeremiah 31:3

With tears streaming down her face in a crowded lobby between church services, she whispered, "But I like women."

Her pain and sincerity were heart-rending! I cannot begin to fathom how such a gentle heart, overflowing with emotion and longing to be loved, has gotten so twisted and out of sync with the heart of a God madly in love with her. Her heavenly Father wants to fulfill her infinitely more than she could ever imagine.

When I first met her, she had shared that she was an atheist. No problem! I love atheists. I love people who have strong convictions, even if they differ with mine. On that first meeting, after I chatted with her and the other girls for an hour and a half, she walked up and gave me a big hug saying, "I hope I didn't offend you when I said I was an atheist!"

Wow! A compassionate atheist who was concerned about offending me. How refreshing! I laughed and assured her she had not.

Now, months later in the church lobby, shattered by conflicting thoughts and feelings, my heart broke as she confessed her overwhelming dilemma. I know only God can clear up her confused identity.

After a few moments of just hugging her as she trembled, I looked into her eyes and said warmly, "I know sweetheart. It's so hard to understand this now, but as God heals your heart from past wounds, you're going to be able to receive His perfect plan for you." I then prayed for her and she went into the next service.

I have no interest in tolerating her, but I am deeply committed to loving her.

I am committed to being there for her as long as she will let me. It is what Jesus does for each of us.

I must do no less.

OFF WITH THEIR HEADS

Everyone is right in his or her own eyes.

Proverbs says it well: "People may be right in their own eyes, but the LORD examines their heart."[14]

Go online and search the name of almost any notable Christian leader, and you will most likely find a mixed bag of comments, accusations, critiques and even slander. There is little grace from some, perhaps well-meaning but at times overly critical individuals, who believe the highest ground is to filet people they don't agree with. This adamant commentary has a take-no-prisoners feel that seems to consider fixing our thoughts on "…what is true, and honorable, and right, and pure, and lovely, and admirable"[15] to be less important than unleashing a torrent of judgment.

It seems the overly divisive "I'm mad as hell, and I'm not going to take it any more" mindset has infected parts of our church family. Talk radio would at times be another in-your-face example of this harsh attitude. If we can't speak the truth in love, what we say may be factual, but can no longer be called the "truth" and represent the God who is truth.[16]

Paul, facing the same contentious spirit once wrote to the Colossian church, "Let your conversation be gracious and attractive so that you will have the right response for everyone."[17] The New King James version translates attractive as, "seasoned with salt." This refers to the word *prudence*, defined as, "acting with or showing care and thought for the future." If our communication with one another bypasses graciousness, kindness and love, what kind of future are we hoping for?

---

14 Proverbs 21:2

15 Philippians 4:8b

16 John 14:6

17 Colossians 4:6

Being right is certainly overrated.

The wisdom of Proverbs aids in our understanding: "Hatred [considering people your enemy] stirs up strife [quarreling, brawling, contention and discord], but love [showing affection, as to a friend] covers all sins [trespasses, apostasy, rebellion, revolts]."[18]

Like the Queen of Hearts in *Alice in Wonderland*, many often rant with an attitude of, "Off with their heads!" forgetting that the head of the Body of Christ, Jesus, came to save, not condemn.[19]

Christ's exhortation toward excessive judgment still applies today: "Then He [Jesus] turned to His critics and asked…'Is this a day to save life or to destroy it?'"[20] The Pharisees were quick to destroy anyone who didn't see the world as they did. Jesus, knowing the effect of their divisiveness, warned them of the consequences of such discord: "What sorrow awaits you teachers of religious law and you Pharisees. Hypocrites! For you cross land and sea to make one convert, and then you turn that person into twice the child of hell you yourselves are!"[21]

Jesus went around doing good and healing.[22]

What are we doing?

---

18 Proverbs 10:12

19 Matthew 18:11 NKJV, John 3:17

20 Mark 3:4b

21 Matthew 23:15

22 Acts 10:38

INTOLERABLE— THE RHETORIC OF ALIENATION

Recently, I asked those attending our church services an interactive question, which they were able to answer anonymously using our remote voting system. I asked, "Do you personally struggle with prejudice toward those in the gay and lesbian lifestyle?"

Our church has grown significantly in the last year. Lots of new people are coming from various backgrounds.

In all of the services, approximately 25 percent admitted that they did indeed struggle with prejudice toward people in such lifestyles. Sadly, it was a higher percentage than I was expecting or hoping for.

I solicited another interactive response to this statement: "I used to struggle with this prejudice, but now I love those in the gay and lesbian lifestyle." An average of 40 percent candidly acknowledged this position.

I then made what I believe was a valid assumption. I said, "Though 25 percent of you are struggling with prejudice toward homosexuals right now, I believe the vast majority of you know this is not where your heart should be. You want to get to the place where you are able to love those in the gay and lesbian lifestyle unconditionally."

No one in the room flinched. Some were perhaps conflicted with their understanding of this level of love, but I'm convinced many in the room, if not all, wanted to love like Jesus loves. But all rooms are not created equal.

Bigotry knows no borders.

> "The practice of tolerance does not mean abandonment or weakening of one's convictions. It means that one is free to adhere to one's own convictions and accepts that others adhere to theirs."
>
> —UNESCO's Declaration on Tolerance

3—ACCEPTING CHURCH

It is neither shy nor isolated.

Prejudice is an intolerable perspective that alienates families and nations. The plague of discrimination spans the globe, seducing all cultures. The stains of religious bigotry have blemished the planet for millennia: from anti-Semitism (prejudice against Jews) to islamophobia (prejudice against Muslims), from hatred of African Americans, to homophobia (prejudice against homosexuals), and of course christophobia (prejudice against followers of Jesus Christ).

Prejudice is alive on planet Earth.

In 1995, UNESCO, an international conference of world leaders further defined the word tolerance: "The practice of tolerance does not mean abandonment or weakening of one's convictions. It means that one is free to adhere to one's own convictions and accepts that others adhere to theirs."[23] UNESCO's Declaration on Tolerance stated the goal of "…harmony in diversity, achieved through mutual respect and understanding."[24]

Even within our global, secular society, true tolerance is seen not as a position of weakness, but of strength. It is viewed as having strength to allow someone else to believe and act differently than I do, without harboring malice or prejudice.

The Bible teaches that before Jesus returns He will once again raise up an accepting church that will reach out in love as He did.[25]

When speaking with the Samaritan woman at the well in John 4, Christ's intention was not to simply ask her for a drink, but, moreover, to freely give her the water that leads to everlasting life. Jesus accepted her, loved her, and didn't hesitate

---

[23] UNESCO—United Nations Educational, Scientific and Cultural Organization Declaration of Principles on Tolerance, Article 1.4—Definition of Tolerance, 1995

[24] UNESCO—United Nations Educational, Scientific and Cultural Organization Declaration of Principles on Tolerance, Article 1.4—Definition of Tolerance, 1995, 27 C/Resolution 5.14

[25] John 13:35

to let her know that He was fully aware of her sin. This same living water freely flows to all today. May we, likewise, offer it as Jesus did to those dying of thirst for the water that leads to everlasting life.

Not only was her sin not a deal-breaker, setting her free from it was the very purpose for which He came. "This is a trustworthy saying, and everyone should accept it: 'Christ Jesus came into the world to save sinners.'"[26]

"…the Son of God came to destroy the works of the devil."[27]

May God weed out of our hearts any lingering prejudice and bigotry toward those He lovingly created in His own image and likeness. May we cover their sin in prayer while embracing and loving them unconditionally. Only then will we demonstrate to a wounded world how He so willingly loves each of us.

THE NON-REACTIONARIES

When the psalmist writes, "Arise, O LORD! Rescue me, my God! Slap all my enemies in the face! Shatter the teeth of the wicked!"[28] or, "You placed my foot on their necks. I have destroyed all who hated me,"[29] or, "Yes, I hate them with total hatred, for Your enemies are my enemies,"[30] I have sometimes wondered, is this attitude the psalmist is expressing really God's heart, or is it just the frustrated cry of a weary soul?

Is this really how the God of love wants His children to relate to those who hate Him and even us?

---

26 1Timothy 1:15

27 1John 3:8b

28 Psalm 3:7

29 Psalm 18:40

30 Psalm 139:22

How do we reconcile the psalmist's hostile response with the seemingly opposing words of Jesus? "You have heard the law that says, 'Love your neighbor' and hate your enemy. But I say, love your enemies! Pray for those who persecute you! In that way, you will be acting as true children of your Father in Heaven. For He gives His sunlight to both the evil and the good, and He sends rain on the just and the unjust alike. If you love only those who love you, what reward is there for that? Even corrupt tax collectors do that much. If you are kind only to your friends, how are you different from anyone else? Even pagans do that. But you are to be perfect, even as your Father in Heaven is perfect."[31]

> **While the anguished cries of the psalmist realistically express raw emotion, they do not necessarily reflect the pristine response of a life thoroughly yielded to God's Spirit.**

Paul, the soon-to-be-martyred apostle, likewise wrote, "Dear friends, never take revenge. Leave that to the righteous anger of God. For the Scriptures say, 'I will take revenge; I will pay them back,' says the LORD."[32]

Is there a conflict between the teachings of these Old and New Testament authors? Or, as reflected in certain verses, just night and day responses to the most challenging of all life's circumstances? Was one reply the not-yet-fully-enlightened reaction of an overwhelmed and legalistic heart and the other the grace-filled response of a heart fully surrendered to the comforting Spirit of God? I have come to the conclusion that while the anguished cries of the psalmist realistically express raw emotion, they do not necessarily reflect the pristine response of a life thoroughly yielded to God's Spirit.

While dying on the cross Jesus modeled how best to respond to those who hate us. He said, "'Father, forgive them, for they

---

31 Matthew 5:43–48

32 Romans 12:19

don't know what they are doing.'"[33] He could have asked for thousands of angels to come to His rescue;[34] He could even have allowed His own heart to be tainted with the same hatred and bitterness of His torturers. Instead, He freely gave His life for them, demonstrating a flawless, yielded response.

This, dear ones, is how Jesus has commanded us to live as well: to love all people at all times, no matter what they may say or do to harm us. Only this response will accurately model the heart of a God who has called us to live as He lived and even to be willing to die as He died. The Bible's challenge to all of us is both inspiring and fulfilling: "Share each other's burdens [load or weight], and in this way obey the law of Christ."[35]

May we each pray as the psalmist did, "Teach me how to live, O Lord. Lead me along the right path, for my enemies are waiting for me."[36]

ABSOLUTELY NO ABSOLUTES

We live in an age marked by the belief that the pinnacle of intelligence is open-mindedness. Our freethinking society often considers it arrogant and narrow-minded to imagine that any viewpoint has greater merit than another. When people emphatically claim to have found a greater truth, they are said to be insensitive to the feelings of others. Therefore, it is the height of presumption to pompously elevate any opinion above another.

Upon closer examination, the rationale and credibility of this so-called nonjudgmental sentiment is both shallow and short-lived.

---

[33] Luke 23:34
[34] Matthew 26:53
[35] Galatians 6:2
[36] Psalm 27:11

More often than not, when an advocate of such is asked to talk about a different point of view, he or she shuts down. The former proponent of tolerance and impartiality feels compelled to adhere to a higher sentiment; one that defends his or her cherished conviction.

> **At last we see the unmasked truth that "absolute tolerance" is by its very definition often intolerant.**

Suddenly, the "open-minded" person views anyone holding a differing opinion as dangerous! He vehemently asserts that having a viewpoint so diametrically opposing the crowd's conviction must be kept out of the dialogue in order to protect the naïve masses from being drawn into such low-minded thought.

What could a person suggest that is so out of step with the perceived good-of-the-culture? Perhaps he asserts that there are absolutes, not just right and wrong, but truth and lies; even that our beliefs on Earth must actually submit to a higher authority, the Creator of all things.

Unthinkable!

The "open-minded" person is absolutely certain that there are no absolutes. One personal preference is not better than another. Ironically, the only person the "open-minded" one sees as evil, is the person who insists that good and evil exist.

Unacceptable!

At last we see the unmasked truth that "absolute tolerance" is by its very definition often intolerant. When pressed to acknowledge what he believes, every person on earth adheres to convictions he believes absolutely, and that must eventually conflict with another point of view.

Like it or not, there are absolutes!

Christian apologist, Gregory Koukl writes, "Most of what passes for tolerance today is not tolerance at all, but rather intellectual cowardice. Those who hide behind the myth of neutrality are often afraid of intelligent engagement. Unwilling to be challenged by alternate points of view, they don't engage contrary opinions or even consider them. It's easier to hurl an insult, "you intolerant bigot"—than to confront the idea and either refute it or be changed by it. 'Tolerance' has become intolerance."[37]

Still the question remains: Are our most cherished convictions true or false? For this highest of all grounds, we should yield to the greatest authority, the most published book of all time—the Holy Bible.

Before dismissing the Bible's content as an antiquated fairy tale, we must be sure we are right. As an atheist, for many years, I mocked the Bible. As a hedonist, I rejected its narrow, puritanical morality as unenlightened. Now, as someone who has diligently studied its wisdom and insight nearly every day since 1972, I've found it to be flawless and absolutely life transforming.

So, what is true tolerance and its value? Christ-followers should afford every person the equal right to choose what he or she believes, as long as it doesn't blatantly harm someone else. But what we cannot afford to do, in a truly reasonable and rational culture, is to embrace every idea as being equally right.

We should love and respect all people. But we must never feel coerced into showing unequivocal respect for ideas and philosophies that injure our spiritual, emotional, mental, and relational wellbeing. Most importantly, we should not befriend those thoughts that conflict with God's best for our lives.

---

[37] Koukl G. The Intolerance of Tolerance. Stand to Reason. Available at http://www.str.org/site/News2?page=NewsArticle&id=5359. Last accessed July 15, 2009.

It requires little tolerance to embrace the convictions of those who agree with us. It takes supernatural grace to love and embrace those who hold convictions that oppose what we believe and know to be true. In fact this is more than tolerance. This is the essence of true love: fully accepting and unconditionally embracing someone else while holding to God's Word.

We are called to offer unconditional love—not unconditional approval.

The Bible clearly illustrates genuine tolerance and understanding when it says, "…don't get involved in foolish, ignorant arguments that only start fights. A servant of the Lord must not quarrel but must be kind to everyone, be able to teach, and be patient with difficult people. Gently instruct those who oppose the truth. Perhaps God will change those people's hearts, and they will learn the truth. Then they will come to their senses and escape from the devil's trap. For they have been held captive by him to do whatever he wants."[38]

> **This is the essence of true love: fully accepting and unconditionally embracing someone else while holding to God's Word.**

We must ask God for His help that we may have this heart—His heart. It may take the patience of Job to demonstrate God's gracious acceptance, but in the end those who are presently spiritually dead or dying will see the God of unconditional love shining through us.

This will make the difference for time and eternity.

---

38 2Timothy 2:23–26

COMPASSION WITHOUT COMPROMISE

Only God can design from emptiness.

Truth and reality stand resolute—whether we believe in them or not. As Paul the great teacher once wrote, "For we can do nothing against the truth, but for the truth."[39]

We cannot create reality—only deception.

So too with the devil! He is the creator of nothing eternal and the counterfeiter of everything pure and holy.

All music was designed by God as a way for creation to worship Him. Lucifer, the defrocked chief musician of heaven, twisted the expression of ecstatic adoration into senseless idolatry and self-worship. He is a shell of his former self, as are the doomed vessels that followed him into nothingness.

In the same way that worship has been deformed and become idolatry, compassion has been perverted and become compromise.

Those who attempt to redefine *compassion*, as "embracing every person's beliefs with love and understanding" will find that reality is not malleable. We cannot conform truth to our image. In the end, we will be conformed to truth. God will either be a stepping-stone guiding us to His one and only reality or, if we choose to cling to our deception, an eternal stumbling block to fantasy. Compromising our spiritual integrity only leads to powerlessness and endless regret. The applause of man is a shallow substitute for our true identity as fearless and compassionate sons and daughters of the living God.

Only God knows what truth is. He will not be intimidated by the angry masses that are invariably wrong. Seductions bring a temporary sense of freedom, but they eventually lead to actual,

---

39 2Corinthians 13:8, NKJV

total bondage. Truth that transforms always requires compassionate courage to do what God intended: to set us free.[40]

Jesus said to the people who believed in Him, "You are truly My disciples if you remain faithful to My teachings. And you will know the truth, and the truth will set you free."

Truth that transforms always requires compassionate courage to do what God intended: to set us free.

Moral and spiritual compromise generates weakness and exploitation.

Scripture emphatically warns us, "Make sure that no one is immoral or godless like Esau, who traded his birthright as the firstborn son for a single meal. You know that afterward, when he wanted his father's blessing, he was rejected. It was too late for repentance, even though he begged with bitter tears."[41] The final battlefields of Earth are laden with the treachery of compromise, where unsuspecting souls will jeopardize the good God has prepared for them by bowing to the momentary adulation of man—nothing more than a warm bowl of beans.

There is coming a day when many in the church will lie in the lap of Delilah, receiving her approval and flattery, while their strength is unwittingly cut off, never to return.

Only character and conviction, based upon God's Word and not man's whim, will bring forth the true joy that lasts forever. The Bible illustrates this crucial principle: "Joyful are people of integrity, who follow the instructions of the LORD. Joyful are those who obey His laws and search for Him with all their hearts. They do not compromise with evil, they walk only in His paths."[42]

The God of compassion alone knows what true compassion looks like. "Is there any encouragement from belonging to

---

40 John 8:31–32

41 Hebrews 12:16–17

42 Psalm 119:1–3

Christ? Any comfort from His love? Any fellowship together in the Spirit? Are your hearts tender and compassionate? Then make me truly happy by agreeing wholeheartedly with each other, loving one another, and working together with one mind and purpose."[43]

Lord, give us Your compassionate, uncompromising heart!

FALSE LOVE

Though God alone is a pure representation of love,[44] we live in a world that vainly attempts to make love a god. Yet, only He can replicate and deposit *True Love* in the hearts of His sincere followers. Only He can define what love is and is not.

Once we reject His perfect plan for us, we become counterfeit creators, attempting to reconstruct our own version of love out of the broken pieces of our lives. The Day of Judgment will reveal both the purity of our motives and the genuineness of our love.

Paul wrote to the Corinthian church, "For we must all stand before Christ to be judged. We will each receive whatever we deserve for the good or evil we have done in this earthly body. Because we understand our fearful responsibility to the Lord, we work hard to persuade others."[45]

John, the beloved disciple of Jesus, provides insight: "This is love, that we walk according to His commandments. This is the commandment, that as you have heard from the beginning, you should walk in it."[46] We cannot model the love God intends for us unless we are following the specific commands He gives us.

---

43 Philippians 2:1–2

44 1John 4:8

45 2Corinthians 5:10–11a

46 2John 6, NKJV

Let's examine the three flavors of false love.

1. False love that thinks it's true but isn't.

Countless love songs, movies and romance novels have been written, attempting to recast true love either as primarily physical or as an emotional connection that has value in and of itself. Each of these superficial representations lack the faithfulness and relational commitment, even covenant, God designed to be the supernatural bond that joins a husband and wife.

The Day of Judgment will reveal both the purity of our motives and the genuineness of our love.

The Bible is clear about God's kind of love: "Give honor to marriage, and remain faithful to one another in marriage. God will surely judge people who are immoral and those who commit adultery."[47]

2. False love that has received true love but doesn't share it.

The principle responsibility for this kind of false love falls at the feet of those who profess to be followers of Jesus Christ but live double lives. While on this Earth, Jesus was very clear as to how we are called to love: "Do to others as you would like them to do to you. If you love only those who love you, why should you get credit for that? Even sinners love those who love them! And if you do good only to those who do good to you, why should you get credit? Even sinners do that much!"[48]

The God of love dared to take true love even further when He presented one of the most important concepts of all time: "Love your enemies! Do good to them. Lend to them without expecting to be repaid. Then your reward from heaven will be very great, and you will truly be acting as children of the Most High, for He is kind to those who are unthankful and wicked. You must be compassionate, just as your Father is compas-

---

47 Hebrews 13:4

48 Luke 6:31–33

sionate."[49] How different would our world be if we were committed to do as Jesus asked us?

Jesus likewise chided the Pharisees saying, "…you ignore justice and the love of God."[50] May we each rise to embrace our glorious calling as ambassadors of the God who alone is love.[51]

3. False love that's desperate but still refuses to love and be loved as God intended.

As an avalanche of deception attempts to redefine truth, lies, good, and evil, so too is there an assault against genuine love, and the relational order God intended. Truth will eventually prevail. However, the interim misrepresentation of the virtue of God's love will clearly separate what is eternally true, from what is a distortion and a lie.

"But those who obey God's Word truly show how completely they love Him. That is how we know we are living in Him."[52]

"Loving God means keeping His commandments, and His commandments are not burdensome."[53]

In the Book of Romans we find perhaps the most chilling section of scripture describing in vivid detail the hollow repercussions of false love. In the years to come, spiritually barren men and women will attempt to remove, discredit, or deny the validity of this portion. But despite their efforts, it will remain the inspired Word of God:

> "So God abandoned them to do whatever shameful things their hearts desired. As a result, they did vile and degrading things with each other's bodies. They traded the truth about God for a lie. So they worshiped and

---

49 Luke 6:35–36

50 Luke 11:42b

51 2Corinthians 5:20

52 1John 2:5

53 1John 5:3

served the things God created instead of the Creator Himself, who is worthy of eternal praise! Amen! That is why God abandoned them to their shameful desires. Even the women turned against the natural way to have sex and indulged in sex with each other. And the men, instead of having normal sexual relations with women, burned with lust for each other. Men did shameful things with other men, and as a result of this sin, they suffered within themselves the penalty they deserved.

"Since they thought it foolish to acknowledge God, He abandoned them to their foolish thinking and let them do things that should never be done."[54]

May we each find the true love that we long for in the arms of the God who alone is capable of loving us with an everlasting love.[55]

THE EXCEPTING CHURCH

Except means, "not included in a category or group."

The Last Days Church will be both an "accepting" and "excepting" church.

As we have discussed in this chapter, we are called and even commissioned by God Himself to accept, with hearts filled with His unconditional love, care and concern, all people outside of the faith, regardless of their sin and struggles.

But the Bible recognizes that hypocrisy amongst those claiming to be followers of Jesus brings a whole different set of challenges and dangers. Living a double life confuses and angers those outside of the church. It says we can say one thing and live another. We have already discussed in detail

---

54 Romans 1:24–28

55 Jeremiah 31:3

the tragic effects this kind of duplicity can bring. But, living a double-minded life likewise causes great confusion and deception to those within the church body as well. Cancerous attitudes and behaviors can spread throughout a healthy body if left unchecked and unchallenged.

This is why Paul wrote so strongly to the Corinthian church when one of its members had fallen into sexual sin with his father's wife (his step-mother). Paul knew that this type of deception could infect the church with other forms of reprehensible behavior.

This would destroy the Christian faith from within.

Paul instructs, in order to prevent such a thing from happening:

> "When I wrote to you before, I told you not to associate with people who indulge in sexual sin. But I wasn't talking about unbelievers who indulge in sexual sin, or are greedy, or cheat people, or worship idols. You would have to leave this world to avoid people like that. I meant that you are not to associate with anyone who claims to be a believer yet indulges in sexual sin, or is greedy, or worships idols, or is abusive, or is a drunkard, or cheats people. Don't even eat with such people.
>
> "It isn't my responsibility to judge outsiders, but it certainly is your responsibility to judge those inside the church who are sinning. God will judge those on the outside; but as the Scriptures say, 'You must remove the evil person from among you.'"[56]

Ray Comfort quotes movie actor Brad Pitt in his book, *What Hollywood Believes*. Pitt, in his youth, was a choirboy raised with "a strong Baptist faith." But in a revealing interview, he shares his spiritual beliefs. Pitt calls religion "…oppression…

---

[56] 1Corinthians 5:9–13

because it stifles any kind of personal individual freedom. I dealt with a lot of that, and my family would diametrically disagree with me on all of that."[57]

About the Parable of the Prodigal Son, Pitt discloses his concept of God: an authoritarian who keeps people in line.

Pitt says, "It is a story which says, if you go out and try to find your own voice and find what works for you and what makes sense for you, then you are going to be destroyed and you will be humbled and you will not be alive again until you come home to the father's ways."[58]

What a sad commentary about such a tenderhearted father, and what a misguided understanding of scripture! Actually, Christ's portrayal of the father in the Parable of the Prodigal Son shows a dad desperately longing for his son's return. The Bible says that the father, filled with love and complete forgiveness, "saw him [the son] while he was yet a great way off."[59]

This compassionate and caring father ran to him, fell upon his neck, kissed him with complete abandon and acceptance in his heart, and rejoiced that his beloved son was safely home. His son had limped home bankrupt and broken. The last thing the father wanted was for his son to be "destroyed." Try as we may to recreate reality, in the end, only the reality of God's will remains forever.

All the father could see was not a rebellious son but rather a damaged life. He was willing to do whatever necessary to restore him. The humbled son immediately embraced this highest level of forgiving love, allowing his elated father to prepare a feast, fully receiving him back into the family.

Christ's portrayal of the father in the Parable of the Prodigal Son shows a dad desperately longing for his son's return.

---

[57] "What Hollywood Believes: An Intimate Look at the Faith of the Famous." by Ray Comfort.
[58] Ibid.
[59] Luke 15:20, NKJV

His return did not engender mere toleration, but love beyond measure.

So too is the heart of our Heavenly Father toward each of us. May we be wise enough to see it and humble enough to receive it.

STORMS ARE COMING

When storms come, we need safe harbors…and storms are coming.

Climate change and global warming will not trigger the tempests that test us most. What should really concern us is that which has the power to change both the spiritual temperature and inner climate of every yielded soul on Earth.

A worldwide revival is coming!

God promises to pour out His Spirit in these Last Days.[60]

Webster rightly defines *revival* as a "return, recall or recovery to life from death or apparent death; as the revival of a drowned person. An awakening of men to their spiritual concerns."[61]

Are we desperate for a "return to life" in our nation?

Do we cry to God for the revival of those who are spiritually dead?

Will we stand in the gap for multitudes free-falling in their self-indulgence?

Will we be ready for this grand opportunity?

Will our churches be safe havens for the weary masses?

---

60 Joel 2:28–29

61 Noah Webster's 1828 American Dictionary

Will our families be flesh and blood representations for those who long to see healthy relationships?

Will our lives provide safety for those dying to live?

This is perhaps the greatest test for every follower of Jesus and the true value of the spiritual maturity and wholeness Christ alone offers.

Am I a safe harbor for people to anchor in public, in private, and without reservation? I'm saddened to know that, at times, I am not.

Am I a safe harbor for people to anchor in public, in private, and without reservation?

It breaks my heart to think my life could actually be a hindrance instead of a help for those around me. But I rejoice in the possibility of living as God intended—that I can and will fulfill God's original intent for my life.

Our capacity to make people feel safe will directly parallel and impact our effectiveness in reaching those overwhelmed by the tsunamis of life. The church as a haven will be key for each of us to be faithful and fruitful in the End Times.

Will people gather or scatter when they come near us?[62] Do we add to their sorrow or relieve their suffering? For Jesus, the answer was clear: "…Jesus went around doing good and healing all who were oppressed by the devil, for God was with Him."[63]

What do we go around doing?

Will God not just be with us, but, more importantly, will we be with God?

The Old Testament raises this poignant question: "When Joshua was near the town of Jericho, he looked up and saw a man standing in front of him with sword in hand. Joshua went

---

62 Mark 12:30, Luke 11:23, NKJV

63 Acts 10:38b

up to him and demanded, 'Are you friend or foe?' 'Neither one,' he replied. 'I am the commander of the Lord's army.' At this, Joshua fell with his face to the ground in reverence. 'I am at your command,' Joshua said. 'What do you want your servant to do?'"[64]

The question is not, "Is God with us?" but, "Are we with God?"

Will we not just live for God, but will we also allow Him to live through us?

It is the most fervent prayer of my heart—that I will know God—to know Him as He longs to be known. This will be the greatest help to others. Am I willing to lay down my life so that I will be an attraction that draws, not a distraction that repels? Only a daily dependence upon Jesus can make this happen. My old life will be of little help.[65]

Will I be safe? Will I allow my heart to remain soft? Will I pay the price to walk in truth and life—to know and be known?

Will I fulfill my destiny as God's hope for this dying world?

"'But you are My witnesses, O Israel!' says the LORD. 'You are My servant. You have been chosen to know Me, believe in Me, and understand that I alone am God. There is no other God—there never has been, and there never will be.'"[66]

The Message Bible says it like this: "You're my handpicked servant, so that you'll come to know and trust Me, understand that I am and who I am. Previous to Me there was no such thing as a god, nor will there be after Me."[67]

---

[64] Joshua 5:13–14

[65] John 6:63

[66] Isaiah 43:10

[67] Isaiah 43:10, The Message

It is both a humbling and compelling reality: we may be the last representation of Jesus Christ others see on this Earth. May we understand, not just the gravity of this divine stewardship, but the awesome privilege. The God of the Universe has created us for this high and holy calling. As we look to Him, He promises that we will reflect the image of the One for whom we were created.[68]

---

[68] 2Corinthians 3:18

QUESTIONS FOR DISCUSSION

1. Have you ever been prejudiced toward any individual or group? Are you presently prejudiced toward any specific segment of our society? (E.g. race, gender, economic status, religious beliefs, sexual preference, etc.) How have any of your prejudices affected others and yourself?

2. Have you felt accepted and loved in the churches you have attended? Or, have you felt conditionally accepted and loved only when you were living up to a set of standards/expectations? How did this affect you and how did you respond?

3. Have you experienced prejudice for being a Christian? How did you respond? How did the response affect others?

4. Have you been able to forgive and love your enemies? If not, what seems to be hindering you from forgiving? How has that impacted your life and the lives of your enemies?

5. What steps are you willing to take today to begin to forgive and love your enemies?

4 TRANSPARENT CHURCH

CHAPTER FOUR

"People say they love truth, but in reality they want to believe that which they love is true."

ROBERT J. RINGER, AMERICAN WRITER

I'm looking for a new kind of leader!

Scripture tells us to "be perfect, even as your Father in heaven is perfect."[1] So we are to show no flaws. Right?

Wrong.

I don't want someone who appears flawless. Everyone who really knows him recognizes he's not.[2]

I don't want an excuse maker. Now is not the time to make excuses. Make a confession, and please don't draw too much attention to yourself.[3]

I can't hear another minimalist message by someone who downplays her faults because she's more concerned about saving face than lying face down before a holy God.[4]

---

1 Matthew 5:48

2 Romans 3:23, 5:12

3 James 5:16

4 Joel 2:17

The "perfection" Matthew 5:48 speaks about cannot be attained by hiding or ignoring flaws. It comes from allowing the strength of God's grace to be perfected through the weakness of my flesh.[5]

I'm really looking for someone who knows how big of a sinner he is; that if it were not for the grace of God, without a doubt, he'd still be drowning in the muck and mire of sin.

I'm hoping for a mentor who knows that his sins ALONE were enough to put the God of the universe on the Cross of Calvary—never mind everyone else's sins.

I'm wanting to hear someone who doesn't have enough time to focus on my sin because she's too busy dissecting her own.

I'm longing for someone like Paul the Apostle, who knew exactly who he was. He said, hands down, he was the worst—a criminal, villainous, the nefarious slug of mankind. He openly admitted, "For I am the least of all the apostles. In fact, I'm not even worthy to be called an apostle after the way I persecuted God's church."[6]

I'm waiting for someone who's absolutely certain, as Paul was, that "'Christ Jesus came into the world to save sinners'—and I am the worst of them all."[7]

I've lost my capacity to listen to a smooth talker, someone who's concerned about protecting her reputation instead of being prepared to lose it—as Jesus willingly did.[8]

I'm dreaming of a leader who, deep down, knows he is no better than anyone else—the first one to hit the altar and often the last to leave. Who gives no less respect to the person who can in no way benefit him than he does to the one who can meet a dire need.

---

[5] 2Corinthians 12:9

[6] 1Corinthians 15:9

[7] 1Timothy 1:15

[8] Philippians 2:7

So what am I looking for?

I'm looking for ME to change!

Transparent Christians must show the heart of God in this critical hour. They must lead by allowing the perfect love of Christ to shine through personal weakness.

In the next phase, the props are all coming down.

Stick figure Christianity is fading away! Nobody's interested. Shallow is stale. Broken is golden—deep is for dinner.

Heaven has prayed for and been granted an indisputable representation of the life of God on the Earth. The passionate Bride of Jesus is rising in resurrection life to shine her brightest at the end of the age.

Admission to this divine incarnation, as always, will be free. But it will cost anyone willing to live the life everything.

Now is the time for leaders to rise like the prophet Joel, crying out: "Let the priests, who minister in the Lord's presence, stand and weep between the entry room to the Temple and the altar. Let them pray, 'Spare your people, LORD!' Don't let your special possession become an object of mockery. Don't let them become a joke for unbelieving foreigners who say, 'Has the God of Israel left them?'"[9]

May those with the courage of the true Israelites of old come forth, those who "…cried out to God during the battle, and he answered their prayer because they trusted in him."[10]

---

9 Joel 2:17

10 1Chronicles 5:20

God, give us fearless fathers like Moses[11] who boldly stood before Pharaoh and later before the rebellious Hebrew children.[12]

Give us those willing to be martyred if necessary, like Queen Esther, who said, "…though it is against the law, I will go in to see the king. If I must die, I must die."[13]

Lord, raise up those bright and shining lights, "…of whom the world [is] not worthy"[14] but whom Heaven will honor for their selfless love.

UNASHAMED NAKEDNESS

Throughout the Bible, God has provided great insight on how to live the victorious Christian life. A particularly profound series of verses that clearly illustrate how we can live as God intended is found in the New Testament letter written by John. He was the disciple who seemed to know best that Jesus loved him.[15]

"This is the message which we have heard from Him and declare to you, that God is light and in Him is no darkness at all. If we say that we have fellowship with Him, and walk in darkness, we lie and do not practice the truth. But if we walk in the light [Greek: "to make known one's thoughts, to be transparent, to break the silence"] as He is in the light, we have fellowship with one another, and the blood of Jesus Christ His Son cleanses us from all sin."[16]

Walking in the light? What a fascinating concept!

---

[11] Exodus 8:12, 15:25, 17:4; Numbers 12:13

[12] Numbers 26:9

[13] Esther 4:16

[14] Hebrews 11:38a, NKJV

[15] John 13:23, 20:2, 21:7, and 21:20

[16] 1John 1:5–7, NKJV (Emphasis mine.)

But how can someone actually walk in the light, as God intended?

The first essential act of faith we each need in order to enjoy an intimate relationship with the God who is Light is admitting our sin before Him. Our transgressions against a holy God are written on our conscience but must be acknowledged in our hearts and, at times, with our mouths.

God is light, and there is no darkness in Him.[17]

He reflects no one but Himself.

He is the Father of lights,[18] who "…lives in light so brilliant that no human can approach Him."[19]

He lives to reflect light, and He longs for His sons and daughters to do the same!

The Message Bible says it this way: "Every desirable and beneficial gift comes out of heaven. The gifts are rivers of life, cascading down from the Father of Light. There is nothing deceitful in God, nothing two-faced, nothing fickle."[20]

Throughout history, God has established proven ways of walking in the light that He has used to foster revivals in the church and awakenings within the culture. We will discuss one, confessing sin, in this section.

> **The first essential act of faith we each need in order to enjoy an intimate relationship with the God who is Light is admitting our sin before Him.**

---

[17] 1John 1:5
[18] James 1:17, NKJV
[19] 1Timothy 6:16
[20] James 1:17, The Message

CONFESS YOUR SINS

Confession of sin can take place in one of four ways:

    a. *Before God*

        Confession of sin must first be offered before the God we have deeply offended by our disobedience.

        The psalmist wrote, "Finally, I confessed all my sins to You and stopped trying to hide my guilt. I said to myself, 'I will confess my rebellion to the LORD.' And You forgave me! All my guilt is gone."[21]

God will lead us at times to confess our sin to a trustworthy, safe person: a proven leader, pastor, or accountability partner.

        The New Testament pattern of confessing sin to God is also clearly established: "If we claim we have no sin, we are only fooling ourselves and not living in the truth. But if we confess our sins to Him, He is faithful and just to forgive us our sins and to cleanse us from all wickedness."[22]

        There is a constant danger of un-confessed sin spreading like a cancer, gradually contaminating every part of our lives: "People who conceal their sins will not prosper, but if they confess and turn from them, they will receive mercy."[23]

    b. *Privately, Before Man*

        God will also, at times, lead us to confess our sins before others.

        "Confess your sins to each other and pray for each other so that you may be healed. The earnest prayer of a righteous person has great power and produces wonderful results."[24]

---

21 Psalm 32:5

22 1John 1:8–9

23 Proverbs 28:13

24 James 5:16

On an individual basis, God will lead us at times to confess our sin to a trustworthy, safe person: a proven leader, pastor, or accountability partner. It is not essential to divulge the gory details unless they are pertinent to our healing. Exercise special care and sensitivity in receiving clear direction from the Holy Spirit regarding both with whom to share and what to confess.

A confession, when executed as God intended, is the testimony that overcomes the world, our flesh, and the devil.

c. *Publically, Before Man*

There are also strategic times when a public confession of past sins before a congregation, within the context of a personal testimony, can bring healing to many in and outside of a church family. As in the case of a private sharing before a safe individual, the content of what we share in public must be Spirit-led.

Having watched people share effectively in this way on a weekly basis for many years now, I realize that a multitude of counsel is helpful in determining what is and is not appropriate. This is especially important if sensitive information is being shared about someone else who will either be present or will hear second-hand what has been shared (e.g., spouses, parents, children, siblings, friends, co-workers, etc.).

Discretion has been defined as, "The ability to avoid words, actions, and attitudes which could result in undesirable consequences."[25] Though I have witnessed first-hand the tremendous value of a Spirit-led public testimony being shared in a humble, vulnerable and unpretentious way, I have also seen on a few occasions feelings being hurt and listeners being offended when less sensitivity and care has been taken.

---

25 Gothard W. Character Qualities. Institute in Basic Life Principles. Available at http://billgothard.com/bill/teaching/characterqualities. Last accessed July 15, 2009.

The Holy Spirit will never humiliate us, but will instead provide the grace necessary to guard the hearts and minds of those sharing and listening. A confession, when executed as God intended, is the testimony that overcomes the world, our flesh, and the devil. "For whatever is born of God overcomes the world. And this is the victory that has overcome the world—our faith."[26]

I believe this principle, in its purest sense, models the supernatural value of the following End Time scripture, which reveals the secret of overcoming the devil and the many formidable challenges ahead: "And they overcame him [the devil] by the blood of the Lamb and by the word of their testimony, and they did not love their lives to the death."[27]

d. *Published*

Throughout history, men and women have courageously shared their deepest struggles and even sins through their writings (e.g., King David, Thomas Aquinas, Madame Guyon, etc.) and, more recently, by means of audio and video. This has brought great comfort and healing to millions through the ages.

The greatest opportunity of all time is now before us. The question becomes, Will we love our lives to the death? Will we boldly and humbly share, with an increasingly skeptical world, God's transforming work in our lives?

As Leonard Sweet, voted one of the most influential Christian leaders in America, writes: "Anyone can show off a revolutionary thought but few people can demonstrate a transformed life."[28]

"Let the redeemed of the Lord say so…"
Psalm 107:2 (NKJV)

---

[26] 1John 5:4, NKJV

[27] Revelation 12:11, NKJV (Emphasis mine.)

[28] Sweet L. *AquaChurch: Essential Leadership Arts for Piloting Your Church in Today's Fluid Culture* (Cook Communications, 2008).

RECIPE FOR REVIVAL

In 1904, a supernatural revival was launched in the nation of Wales that spread around the world. Within two years, 5,000,000 people became Christ followers worldwide. In Atlantic City, New Jersey, with a population of 60,000, only 50 adults were reported unconverted.

One of the catalysts for this Welsh Revival was a young man named Evan Roberts. Winkie Pratney, in his classic book, *Revival*, describes Roberts' commitment to transparency in the church. Having seen enormous breakthroughs in the Spirit realm, Roberts relayed four conditions he found necessary for God to revive the church and awaken the culture:[29]

1. The past must be clear, every sin must be confessed to God, and any wrong must be put right to man.

Our link to past sin is the greatest hindrance to the future release of God's Spirit. Blockages to the flow of God's Spirit in us will eventually obstruct the release of His Spirit to those around us.

Is there any lingering sin that you need God to forgive? Any broken relationship that needs restoration? I pray I don't look back from heaven and see that God could have been released in my life to do mighty things if I had just been willing to clear my past, confess my sin, and restore the broken relationships in my life.

My mother was a prayer warrior! During the later years of her life, she prayed four to five hours a day. Alone, and without anyone influencing this hidden dimension of her life, she daily lifted up hundreds of individuals before the throne of grace. As a direct result of her prayers, I received Jesus as my Lord and Savior on Mother's Day, 1972. Within 18 months, my two brothers and two sisters had each likewise surrendered their lives to Jesus. To this day, all of us would say that our mother's

---

[29] Pratney W. *Revival: Principles to Change the World* (Christian Life Books, 2002).

intercessory prayers are the single greatest factor resulting in our presently serving the purposes of God.

In 2008, my four siblings and I went on a pilgrimage to our ancestral home of Sicily. Our father and grandparents were born there. The goal of the trip was to break any ancestral hindrances, sins, or even curses that may have been passed on generationally from our forebears. Those who are aware of the roots of the Mafia in Sicily or have seen the Godfather movies won't find it hard to imagine how there could be lingering strongholds!

God can give us the necessary grace to break the link that keeps us bound to that which saps our strength and prohibits the life He intended.

On our very focused two-week journey, we spent hours itemizing every sinful dimension or area of bondage in our ancestors' lives that we were aware of. Our journey together was a very intense, revealing and painful time. Highly introspective and reflective discussions, prayer, and tears propelled us into deep realms of confession and of asking forgiveness from God and one another. We actually went to the cemeteries in the hometowns of our ancestors and, with these detailed lists of sins, confessed and prayed for God to break any generational curses that scripture teaches can be passed on to the third and even fourth generations.[30]

Though on Earth we may never know the eternal fruit of these painful days of processing, my family is convinced that roots of deception and seduction were ripped out, and eternal seeds of humility, healing, and purity were planted.

2. Everything doubtful must be removed from our lives once and for all.

Are there ongoing links to past sins and present bondages in our lives that need to be broken? Have we kept the door to past corruption open? God can give us the necessary grace

---

[30] Exodus 34:7, Numbers 14:18, Deuteronomy 5:9

to break the link that keeps us bound to that which saps our strength and prohibits the life He intended.

I believe, if we will ask, the Holy Spirit will point out the portals of compromise that prevent the free flow of God's life in us.[31]

3. Prompt, implicit, and unquestioning obedience to the Holy Spirit.

Every call to stand in faith requires action. It is the difference between a deal-maker and a deal-breaker with the God of faith. As the Bible assures it is impossible to please God without faith,[32] so too, we are not actually walking by faith without evident acts of faith.[33] Like hope and love, faith is an action word.

4. Public confession of Christ.

The Word of God is clear that we hold the keys of life and death in the words that we either courageously speak or tragically choose not to.[34]

"For I am not ashamed of this Good News about Christ. It is the power of God at work, saving everyone who believes…"[35]

"But how can they call on Him to save them unless they believe in Him? And how can they believe in Him if they have never heard about Him? And how can they hear about Him unless someone tells them?"[36]

There's a time to speak and a time to be silent.[37] May we each discern which is needed, for it certainly will make an eternal difference.

---

31 Matthew 7:7, Luke 11:9

32 Hebrews 11:6a

33 James 2:20,26

34 Proverbs 18:21

35 Romans 1:16a

36 Romans 10:14

37 Ecclesiastes 3:7

BOLDLY BROKEN

"We are a thin film of thought confined to a narrow band around an undistinguished planet orbiting a pretty average star."

BRYAN APPLEYARD[38]

Reality is by its very nature humbling.

We should never think too highly of ourselves. It is God who gives us value. Aside from Him, we are nothing special.

It is a most extraordinary miracle that Paul, the one who humbly acknowledged, "…Christ Jesus came into the world to save sinners, of whom I am chief,"[39] would also be able to write, "…Christ Jesus our Lord, in whom we have boldness and access with confidence through faith in Him."[40]

His gross sin had not disqualified him, but instead positioned him to receive the grace that fully accepts without reservation. The word *boldness* here literally means, "the confidence of full self-disclosure without fear, the freedom to speak one's heart and mind that is rooted in the full acceptance of the One listening." God longs for us to walk in a boldness that gives us liberty to run to Him even though He knows we are broken and bruised. God has never done anything to intentionally draw us away from Him, but always toward Him.

With this understanding of confession of sin in mind, let's examine the second proven dimension of walking in the light that God has used in revivals and awakenings throughout history.

---

[38] Appleyard B. Nature in its Infinite Power asks an Awkward Question. The Sunday Times. January 2, 2005. Available at http://www.timesonline.co.uk/tol/comment/article407699.ece. Last accessed July 15, 2009.

[39] 1Timothy 1:15, NKJV

[40] Ephesians 3:11b–12, NKJV (Emphasis mine.)

BE TRANSPARENT

Honesty is one of the premiere values buried deep within the heart of this generation. They feel lied to by parents, peers, teachers, the media, the government, and even the church. A highly suspicious society has all but given up trusting anyone and anything. It desperately wants the truth. So jaded by lies, it can readily smell counterfeits. Attempts to reach these doubting souls must drip with reality. Raw, real and unrehearsed testimonies, welling up from spirit-filled depths, and costing everything, are what will work in the days ahead.

The man who affected me the most in my young life was Dr. Martin Luther King, Jr. I was nineteen when he was murdered at just thirty-nine years old. I cried for days. Because of how he lived and died, within three months of his assassination, I spent the summer living among inner city black youth. While still in college, I would spend the next summer doing the same.

I wasn't even a follower of Jesus. As a matter of fact, I was an in-your-face atheist. But I didn't see him as a religious leader; I saw him as an honest father. I was so desperately hungry for the unfiltered truth that I would have followed him anywhere.

I didn't want religion. I wanted reality.

With this in mind, consider the Apostle John's profound insight as to how we can reach those in darkness and walk in the light in our day:

"But if we walk in the light [Greek: "to make known one's thoughts, to be transparent, to break the silence"] as He is in the light, we have fellowship with one another, and the blood of Jesus Christ His Son cleanses us from all sin."[41]

"To make known our thoughts, to be transparent, and to break the silence"—this is a perfect description of the essential qual-

---

41 1John 1:7, NKJV (Emphasis mine.)

> **Hiding the truth can cause as much damage as living a lie.**

ities needed to effectively share what Jesus has done in our lives. It is the key to reaching a culture that has been hyped to death. Let's take a closer look at this definition of "walking in the light."

Make Known Your Thoughts—"Has the LORD redeemed you? Then speak out! Tell others He has redeemed you from your enemies."[42] Hiding the truth can cause as much damage as living a lie.

Be Transparent—Jesus said, "…the ruler of this world is coming, and he has nothing in Me."[43] In other words, Jesus was saying, I have power over the devil because I am not living a double life—what you see is what you get.

Break the Silence—The word testimony in Revelation 12:11 is the Greek word *maturia*, meaning "evidence given, a record or report." This is derived from *martus*, from which comes the word martyr. In the truest sense, sharing the depth of our past or present pain and the details of God's miraculous rescue will cost us dearly, but will reap truly eternal rewards.

When Adam and Eve first walked with their Creator the Bible says, "…they were both naked, the man and his wife, and were not ashamed [disappointed, confounded, or confused]."[44]

There was nothing to hide and no one to hide from.

During this most innocent of ages, the first couple had no knowledge of evil, as Eve had not yet been deceived and Adam had not yet rebelled. But soon they would know the inevitable pain of deception and rebellion.

Hiding beneath fig leaves was the unavoidable result of abandoning their true covering: the God who alone is able to cover

---

42 Psalm 107:2

43 John 14:30, NKJV

44 Genesis 2:25, NKJV

and protect us. Since that tragic moment, the only protection we have against evil is our willful re-submission to the perfect plan and purpose of God. Only our Maker can restore the security He intended for us. Without a continuous allegiance to the Lord of all, we will again be enticed into exchanging the genuine freedom of knowing God for the fleeting and unfulfilling pleasures of sin.

At a checkout stand in an electronics store in Rome, Italy, I saw an advertisement for pornographic software. It read, "There's nothing to hide. The only sin is to not view it." How utterly ridiculous! The devil knows the best defense against purity is a seductive offense. If we make denial a way of life, hardening our hearts inevitably leads to a dead conscience.[45]

The seductive serpent in the Garden of Eden encouraged Eve to eat the forbidden fruit saying, "You won't die! … God knows that your eyes will be opened as soon as you eat it, and you will be like God, knowing both good and evil."[46] Thousands of years later, we still hear this insidious lie: You can be your own god! This foolish fabrication will eventually be exposed for what it is.

The original intention of a fully revealed Creator is that each of us lives honest and open lives, hiding nothing from God or from one another. The Church of the future will boldly rise to fully embrace this challenge of transparency.

Identification and not persuasion will change hearts in the 21st Century.

Perhaps Jesus Himself spoke the clearest identification verse in the Bible when He said, "And I know that His command is everlasting life. Therefore, whatever I speak, just as the Father has told Me, so I speak."[47] Even Paul the great Apostle understood the importance of passionately and transparently

---

45 1 Timothy 4:2

46 Genesis 3:4-5

47 John 12:50

sharing his life with others: "…for which I am an ambassador in chains; that in it I may speak boldly, as I ought to speak."[48]

The pure in heart will see God![49]

Those who hunger and thirst for what is right will be filled.[50]

Everyone who overcomes in this life will eat from the tree of life, which is in the midst of the paradise of God.[51]

SHAMELESS

Ever since Adam and Eve fell into sin, the grace to be naked without shame is gone—except, of course, for babies and toddlers.

Yet, more than ever before, multitudes willingly pay the significant price of admission to behold nakedness. Though morally treacherous to dabble in, men and women, sons and daughters, even dads and moms uncover themselves. Customers pay to the tune of billions of dollars to view nudity on the Internet, cable television, in movie theaters, and on stages around the world. And, aside from those billions of dollars, the "cost" to those seducing and being seduced is exorbitant. Their notoriety will be short-lived. Once the flower has faded and the beauty of youth is exhausted, they too will be thrown onto the cultural ash heap. The devil doesn't recycle. He just destroys and discards.

The false feeling of intimacy that they offer is a shallow substitute for the guilt-free relationship God longs to have with each of us. Try as we may, there is no replacement for the void only God can fill. Some will call it a "manufacturer's flaw," but

---

[48] Ephesians 6:20
[49] Matthew 5:8
[50] Matthew 5:6
[51] Revelations 2:7

I trust the Bible's account first and foremost: "...for Thou hast created all things, and for Thy pleasure they are and were created."[52] I have found no greater pleasure in life than the breathtaking realization that my life actually pleases God!

Only honesty can resurrect innocence.

So, how can the guilt and shame of innocence lost be restored?

Is there a redeemed dimension of nakedness that we, as followers of Jesus Christ, can experience?

Absolutely, there is!

On a physical level, the God who invented sex was not naive to its attraction, power and fulfillment. For decades now, surveys have shown that those who experience the greatest sexual fulfillment are heterosexual, married couples who are faithful in their monogamous relationship. This kind of sex, and the nakedness that being physically intimate necessitates, is as God designed it to be: simultaneously wonderful, exhilarating and satisfying.

On both an emotional and spiritual level, this principle is the same. We must first be naked before an all-knowing God. Though our tendency is to hide like Adam and Eve, it's obvious that God sees and knows everything about us. Nothing can be hidden from our omniscient Creator. The Bible makes this quite clear when it states, "Nothing in all creation is hidden from God. Everything is naked and exposed before His eyes, and He is the one to whom we are accountable."[53]

Only honesty can resurrect innocence.

True healing comes when we are humble enough to bare our soul and admit to God, "Against You, and You alone, have I

---

52 Revelation 4:11b, KJV

53 Hebrews 4:13

sinned; I have done what is evil in Your sight. You will be proved right in what You say, and Your judgment against me is just."[54]

BLOOD AND GUTS

It's awkward for most people to be even partially naked in front of someone else. We've all been in a high school gym class. I don't cherish the memory of the communal showers during my six years of boarding school. Though my more recent doctor appointments have been less embarrassing, they are still quite uncomfortable. Most of us can relate to a racing heart while sitting on an examination table in nothing but a simulated cotton gown and then hearing the snap of a latex glove. Oi!

Nakedness is embarrassing.

Even as a former hippie, I can still remember many humiliating moments trying to be cool and naked at the same time. It just never seemed to work. If you don't believe me, you can ask Ezekiel, who lied naked on his side for 390 days in a row.[55] Talk about mortifying.

But the naked truth, transparent vulnerability, is an essential part of emotionally connecting when ministering to others, whether it is sharing with one person or one hundred.

Preaching has been described as "standing before a congregation and opening a vein." It has been rightly, though perhaps somewhat indelicately, surmised: "If there is little blood, there is little guts."

The best messages or testimonies are often those that cost the communicator the most. That's why the Bible is the most vulnerable book of all time. It is shocking to consider how much it

---

54 Psalm 51:4, 55

55 Ezekiel 4:9

cost the 40 authors of the Bible to speak so forthrightly about their fears, weaknesses, and even sins.

Someone once said that the Bible has to be inspired by God because no one would talk about his or her heroes in such an unflattering way.

Similarly, no one would divulge their embarrassing shortcomings and serious misdeeds without the comforting assurance that it pleases God and helps those listening. If we pay the price of going deep by being candid about our weaknesses and mistakes, others, in return, can be forthright about their own struggles.

I have known a man named Lou Engle since 1989. We were elders together for four years in the early 90's, in a local church in Los Angeles pastored by Che Ahn. During this significantly challenging season, we shared many hours of vulnerable accountability in a small group of leaders. Our deepest struggles were candidly and regularly verbalized. Words of encouragement and exhortation flowed freely during these exposed exchanges.

Though I would only see Lou periodically after our years together, we had been through enough profoundly moving times of prayer, confession and nakedness in the presence of God, that an irreplaceable bond had been established.

Over the past decade God has used Lou and Che mightily to spearhead gatherings of thousands of believers for consecrated days of prayer and fasting. These holy convocations, known as "The Call," have taken place in major cities around the world, and have been primary catalysts in promoting global intercession.

Recently, I ran into Lou at a conference. We hadn't seen each other in a while and so purposed to spend some time together. We had barely sat down, and before any other discussion

> **He had too much to lose to hide. Instead he turned himself in at every appropriate opportunity.**

had taken place, Lou began to share with me about the struggles he had encountered over the past few years. He elaborated in highly personal detail the great inner wrestling he often experienced. It was undoubtedly awkward, both for him to share and for me to hear, but he communicated without any pretense or self-protection. His life wasn't spiraling out of control, but he was vigilantly standing guard over all he had been entrusted.

Lou had learned long ago that toxic secrets can kill you. With a beautiful wife of many years and eight precious children, he had too much to lose to hide. Instead he turned himself in at every appropriate opportunity. It was so authentic and refreshing I wanted to cry. No wonder God is using him in such significant ways.

Numerous verses throughout the Bible elaborate this wonderful principle of genuineness. Consider the marvelous implications of these profound truths:

> "An honest answer is like a kiss of friendship."
> *Proverbs 24:26*

> "...the honest will inherit good things."
> *Proverbs 28:10b*

> "If you are faithful in little things, you will be faithful in large ones. But if you are dishonest in little things, you won't be honest with greater responsibilities."
> *Luke 16:10*

> "Don't think you are better than you really are. Be honest in your evaluation of yourselves, measuring yourselves by the faith God has given us. Just as our bodies have many parts and each part has a special function, so it is with Christ's body. We are many parts of one body, and we all belong to each other."
> *Romans 12:3b–5*

"We tell the truth before God, and all who are honest know this."
2Corinthians 4:2b

"You yourselves are our witnesses—and so is God—that we were devout and honest and faultless toward all of you believers."
1Thessalonians 2:10

Lord, make us genuine representations of those rescued by a loving God!

HEAVEN'S COMING TO EARTH

There is nothing more exciting than considering the extraordinary blessings "…God has prepared for those who love Him. But it was to us that God revealed these things by His Spirit. For His Spirit searches out everything and shows us God's deep secrets."[56]

Each day we are drawing closer to the end of the age and the fullness of time when God will announce the promised new Heaven and new Earth.[57] God's Spirit is removing the veil of un-enlightenment and revealing all that awaits us in Heaven. Though much is still unknown, what has been disclosed is truly captivating.

"For we know in part and we prophesy in part. But when that which is perfect has come, then that which is in part will be done away. For now we see in a mirror, dimly, but then face to face. Now I know in part, but then I shall know just as I also am known."[58]

---

[56] 1Corinthians 2:9b–10

[57] Revelation 21:1

[58] 1Corinthians 13:9–10, 12, NKJV

> **We will see God face to face, and then at last we will know who He is, and whom we were meant to be.**

In this immature, temporary dimension on Earth, we can feel and understand only within limits. But when we come into our mental and moral completeness in Heaven, we will feel and understand perfectly and be as acutely aware of one another as God is of us.

The above verses in 1 Corinthians 13 indicate that in Heaven we will know as fully as we are known. The hereafter will be an atmosphere permeated with maximum disclosure, where each of us will be thoroughly revealed. There will be no more masks, no facades, and no hidden faces. Just One face! We will see God face to face, and then at last we will know who He is, and whom we were meant to be.

Am I saying that we will know each other's sins and weaknesses in Heaven?

Absolutely!

But not in the scandalous way we can sometimes be aware of one another's shortcomings on Earth. We will fully discern that someone had an addiction, or was susceptible to a certain temptation. But in the presence of God's unconditional love, there will be no impression of judgment, no feeling of superiority or inferiority, and certainly no condescension or condemnation.

In a sense, looking at our past challenges will be like examining a giant redwood tree that has been sawn in half and laid on its side. Its inner growth rings tell the tale of surviving fires, withstanding floods, or resisting myriads of insects who ravaged the giant tree.

But in eternity, beyond the perils of Earth, there will be no sense of distress, just instantaneous insight, compassion and understanding.

As the Bible says, "The temptations in your life are no different from what others experience."[59] In Heaven, at last, we will see instantly how every one of us has struggled in similar areas. There will no longer be the veil of self-righteous positioning or of self-defeating comparison, where one person vainly assumes that his or her sins were more or less than someone else's. At last, it is infinitely clear:

> **There will no longer be the veil of self-righteous positioning or of self-defeating comparison.**

We all sinned!

We all needed God to save us!

We have all been forgiven!

Let's party!

The comparison game will be over. We will see clearly that the ground is even at the Cross. I am no better than anyone else—and no worse. We will not have to dialogue to find out who each other is: what we have done, where we have been, or who we really are. It will all be self-evident.

So, why would any of this be important in the here and now of Earth?

For one absolutely essential and startling reason:

Jesus prayed to His Father, "May Your Kingdom come soon. May Your will be done on earth as it is in heaven."[60] In other words, "Father, may Your will be done in Me and through Me, as You originally intended in the Garden, and as will eventually be completed in the New Heaven and New Earth."

---

59 1Corinthians 10:13a

60 Matthew 6:10

Heaven longs to come to Earth. It will not be denied. Whatever is happening in Heaven is not just destined to replicate here; it is actually the will of the Father that it does come today, not at some belated, future date.

When Heaven touches our lives, we always long for more. When Earth distracts from Heaven, we settle for as little as possible. Until Heaven comes to Earth, we will long for more or live for less. Everything good on Earth is in some way a reflection of Heaven. Everything bad on Earth is in some way Heaven distorted. Heaven wants to come to Earth—NOW! The question is, will we let it?

QUESTIONS FOR DISCUSSION

1. What encounter with genuineness has touched or changed your life?

2. Are you open and transparent about your areas of weakness and temptation? If not, what seems to hinder you from being transparent? If you are transparent, how has this decision affected your life and those you have shared with?

3. Have you ever been a part of a church that practiced transparency? If yes, how did it impact your life? If no, how has that affected you?

4. Is there something hidden in your life that you need to share with someone safe? If so, what seems to be hindering you from sharing? What do you think would happen if you shared?

5. Have the links to past sins in your life been broken? If so, how has this affected your life and your relationships? If not, how would your life be different if they were broken?

5 DISCERNING CHURCH

CHAPTER FIVE

"Do not go where the path may be.
Go instead where there is no path, and leave a trail."
RALPH WALDO EMERSON

Do good and evil actually exist, and is there still a need to discern the difference? Has our 21st Century culture somehow been liberated from the need to distinguish truth from lies?

Noah Webster, the original author of the classic reference tool, Noah Webster's 1828 American Dictionary, defines the word discern, "to see or understand the difference…between good and evil, truth and falsehood." You would think such a straightforward definition would stand the test of time. But as revisionists have been busy reinventing history, so have academic pundits recast the word discern in their own image.

The repackaged meaning of discern in the 2008 version of the Merriam-Webster Dictionary now defines it: "to recognize or identify right from wrong." Hmm? Was this verbal slight-of-hand a significant alteration, or an acceptable summation of the same word?

Without the moral compass of good, evil, truth and lies, who determines what is right and what is wrong? Should such conclusions be left up to each individual's discretion, or the whim of the masses?

> **The greatest deception the devil ever perpetrated was convincing people that he doesn't exist.**

Having considered the ramifications of these questions, it seems obvious that the word discern has been stripped of its essence, all that Noah Webster intended. With the decisive nouns—good, evil, truth and falsehood extracted from the definition, we are left with the fluid impulse of personal preference, a completely subjective reality, which has no resemblance to absolute truth at all. Each person may create his or her own version of good, evil, truth and lies.

This supposed "new and improved" definition of discern is ironically totally lacking in discernment. At best, it's the perfect recipe for deception: the only possible outcome of man playing God. Unless we are acutely aware that good and evil and their counterparts, truth and lies, exist, we will eventually be snared by evil and consigned to live a lie.

The greatest deception the devil ever perpetrated was convincing people that he doesn't exist.

At one point, in the Garden of Eden, all Adam and Eve knew was good. They weren't alone. All that God had made was good: the light, the land and water, the grass, herbs, and fruit, the fish and birds, the wild animals and livestock. It was all good![1]

Yet, in the middle of this majestic garden, the potential for unrestrained sin lay dormant. A deceitful act of treachery, and another of rebellion, awakened unprecedented evil among men and women. These two alternate realities co-existed in the first dwelling of human kind. One was found in the Tree of Life. Adam and Eve feasted daily upon the fruit of a blessed relationship with their Creator.

The other was the Tree of the Knowledge of good and evil—an option bearing fruit which God had forbidden.

---

1 Genesis 1:4, 10, 12, 21, 25, 31

This was the life-altering test our first-parents ultimately failed.

The same two very distinct choices remain today.

True freedom must always provide the ability to choose. But the consequences of our decisions will reveal our true heart. In the end, God alone, as the author and Creator of all things, determines the eternal value of everything that exists. He will even determine the merit of our decisions: whether they are good or evil, the truth or a lie, right or wrong.

> **True freedom must always provide the ability to choose.**

And God's definitions need no revision.

A HEARING HEART

The word of the Lord has always been precious.

During the childhood of the prophet Samuel, "…the word of the LORD was rare in those days; there was no widespread revelation."[2]

Speaking for God, the prophet Amos wrote, "'The time is surely coming,' says the Sovereign LORD, 'when I will send a famine on the land—not a famine of bread or water but of hearing the words of the LORD. People will stagger from sea to sea and wander from border to border searching for the word of the LORD, but they will not find it.'"[3]

During the first nine years of my relationship with Jesus, I struggled with discerning the voice of God. Then in 1981, God told me He wanted me to teach His people how to hear His voice. His invitation was not an audible voice, but it was a distinct impression that I knew was God's Spirit.

---

2 1Samuel 3:1b

3 Amos 8:11–12

Hearing and obeying God is essential in this age of unprecedented challenges, economic uncertainty, spiritual warfare, and acute deception.

I was stunned!

I shot back, "But God, I know nothing about how to hear Your voice." His immediate response was, "That is why I'm asking you. I want to train you, so you can train others." This launched an intense two-year season of fasting and prayer, in which I dissected the New Testament, examining the Biblical patterns of hearing and obeying God's Spirit. He began to show me, in great detail, the secrets of hearing His voice. Subsequently, I traveled extensively conducting seminars on hearing God.

Hearing and obeying God is essential in this age of unprecedented challenges, economic uncertainty, spiritual warfare, and acute deception.

It is obvious that we must discern God's will before we can do it.

We must know His heart before we can live it.

We must hear God's voice before we can speak for Him.

If we are brutally honest with ourselves we realize, we know so little. That's why James, the brother of Jesus, wrote, "If you need wisdom, ask our generous God, and He will give it to you. He will not rebuke you for asking."[4]

Yet Jesus emphatically proclaimed, "My sheep listen to My voice; I know them, and they follow Me."[5] Paul likewise wrote, "For all who are led by the Spirit of God are children of God."[6] Not that we are made children of God by being led, but that those who are walking in the life and authority as sons and daughters of God are led by His Spirit.

---

[4] James 1:5
[5] John 10:27
[6] Romans 8:14

When God asked King Solomon what he wanted most, the humble king replied "an understanding, hearing heart."[7]

God is asking the same question today.

What is our answer?

What do we believe we are capable of being and doing without hearing His voice above all others?

Jesus was even clear about His own limitations on Earth, "I tell you the truth, the Son can do nothing by Himself. He does only what He sees the Father doing. Whatever the Father does, the Son also does."[8]

If Jesus needed to be led by His heavenly Father, how much more do we?

Above all else, we must learn to hear and obey God's voice. His primary means of speaking to us is through Scripture,[9] but He can also communicate with us in ways consistent with His Word.

Unless truth is based upon the eternal Word of God, the Holy Bible, in due course it will deteriorate into apostasy.

As Moses said, "You will be blessed if you obey the commands of the LORD your God that I am giving you today. But you will be cursed if you reject the commands of the LORD your God and turn away from Him and worship gods you have not known before."[10]

May we receive the blessing and reject the curse.

---

7 1Kings 3:9
8 John 5:19
9 2Peter 1:19
10 Deuteronomy 11:27–28

THE APOSTATE CHURCH

Deception gets a facelift with each successive generation.

Repackaged for the times, it struts on stage acting as if what we've been waiting for has finally arrived.

It insists: "Why buy an old, outdated version of lies, when you can have a newer, contemporary edition?" Yet, "…history merely repeats itself. It has all been done before. Nothing under the sun is truly new."[11] No amount of time can transform lies into truth. The substance of every deception remains the same: it is birthed in Hell,[12] and to Hell it will inevitably be consigned.[13] Unless truth is based upon the eternal Word of God, the Holy Bible, in due course it will deteriorate into apostasy.

The root meaning of apostasy is "to depart or defect."[14]

God's Word is truth![15] Any philosophy or ideology that attempts to contradict the Word of God must be discarded or it will become an intellectual cancer. The serpent in the Garden so fraudulently promised, "You won't die!"[16] Many are still foolishly buying into this tragic lie of catastrophic consequence. It is a fatal distraction.

The devil couldn't deliver on his promise back then, and he certainly can't fulfill it now. Jesus passionately warned us, "What sorrow awaits you who are praised by the crowds, for their ancestors also praised false prophets."[17]

For all five years while attending a secular university I was an atheist, hedonist, and anarchist. I was a dedicated disciple of humanism. Not surprisingly, during that hopeless period of

---

[11] Ecclesiastes 1:9

[12] John 8:44

[13] Revelation 20:10

[14] Noah Webster defined apostasy as "an abandonment of what one has professed; a total desertion, or departure from one's faith or religion."

[15] Psalm 119:160, John 17:17

[16] Genesis 3:4a

[17] Luke 6:26

time, I became suicidal for six months, daily wishing for death. It is only by the grace of God, and my mother's prayers, that I survived.

Since that depressing time, I have fully immersed my life in God's perfect Word and found it to be flawlessly true. As the Holy Bible so clearly states, "All Scripture is inspired by God and is useful to teach us what is true and to make us realize what is wrong in our lives. It corrects us when we are wrong and teaches us to do what is right."[18]

Unless we yield to the Bible's timeless wisdom we will one day find ourselves held captive by deceptive lies, each rendering grave and lasting consequences.

Remember the words of Paul the Apostle. Once totally deceived, but thankfully rescued to live a life filled with truth, he wrote, "For I am jealous for you with the jealousy of God Himself. I promised you as a pure bride to one Husband—Christ. But I fear that somehow your pure and undivided devotion to Christ will be corrupted, just as Eve was deceived by the cunning ways of the serpent. You happily put up with whatever anyone tells you, even if they preach a different Jesus than the one we preach, or a different kind of Spirit than the one you received, or a different kind of gospel than the one you believed."[19]

Paul knew all too well the frightening repercussions of believing a lie. Once delivered, he spent the remainder of his life fighting evil with the truth of God's Word. For taking this valiant stand, he said, "And now the prize awaits me—the crown of righteousness, which the Lord, the righteous Judge, will give me on the day of His return. And the prize is not just for me but for all who eagerly look forward to His appearing."[20]

---

18 2Timothy 3:16

19 2Corinthians 11:2–4

20 2Timothy 4:8

HERE COMES THE SIGN

God is speaking!

Are we listening?

The writer of the Book of Hebrews challenged all true believers that he had depths of profound truth to share with them about Jesus,[21] but "…you are spiritually dull and don't seem to listen.[22] You are like babies who need milk and cannot eat solid food. For someone who lives on milk is still an infant and doesn't know how to do what is right. Solid food is for those who are mature, who through training have the skill to recognize the difference between right and wrong."[23]

The New King James version translates verse 14 in this way, "But solid food belongs to those who are of full age, that is, those who by reason of use have their senses exercised to discern both good and evil."[24]

These scriptures could be accurately paraphrased, "I would love to talk with you more about knowing Jesus, but you have become dull of hearing. True maturity belongs to those who have developed a spiritual sensitivity to discern what is good and God, and what is evil and not God—what is His leading and what is not."

True maturity belongs to those who have developed a spiritual sensitivity to discern what is good and God, and what is evil and not God.

Learning to hear God's voice is a spiritual exercise of submitting our heart, mind and will to yield to the slightest promptings of the Holy Spirit. As we build these Spirit-muscles, He can then lead us throughout our lives, moment by moment.

---

21 Hebrews 5:1–10

22 "because you have become dull of hearing'" NKJV

23 Hebrews 5:11, 12b–14

24 Hebrews 5:14, NKJV

In the Old Testament, God led the children of Israel with "...a pillar of cloud by day and...a pillar of fire by night."[25]

Only then can we live as, "...His workmanship, created in Christ Jesus for good works, which God prepared beforehand that we should walk in them."[26] This Spirit-led lifestyle is exactly what God intended for each of us, from eternity past into everlasting life.

But what are the indications of God's leading? The Book of James provides a clear sequence to process the wisdom of the Holy Spirit: "But the wisdom that is from above is first pure, then peaceable, gentle, willing to yield, full of mercy and good fruits, without partiality and without hypocrisy. Now the fruit of righteousness is sown in peace by those who make peace."[27]

Each day we have numerous opportunities to allow the blood of Jesus to purify our hearts. Only then can we enjoy the life-transforming peace of knowing we are truly loved and forgiven. With pure hearts and God's peace abiding in us, His Spirit will begin to gently lead and guide each of our lives. If we are willing to yield, and if our hearts have received the mercy and forgiveness of God, then we will be able to live in the fruit of God's Spirit.

Following this profound pattern of receiving wisdom, these verses offer two additional safeguards and cautions that, if observed, will keep us flowing in the peace of God and away from confusion. We must not presume to know what God's will is, without a constant dependence upon Him to lead. Any personal preference will eventually dissipate into partiality, which will lead us away from God's best.

The second defense against deception is guarding our hearts from all hypocrisy. The Psalmist describes the folly of living a less than honest life before God, "If I had not confessed the

---

[25] Exodus 13:22, Numbers 14:14, Deuteronomy 1:33

[26] Ephesians 2:10, NKJV

[27] James 3:17–18, NKJV

No leading is too small and insignificant, if it is indeed God speaking.

sin in my heart, the Lord would not have listened."[28] James adds, "…a double-minded man, (is) unstable in all his ways."[29] And Paul challenges, "…let the peace that comes from Christ rule (umpire, decide, direct) in your hearts."[30]

As God's peace directs our lives, His leading has been described in various ways:

- an inner voice or urging
- an exceptionally clear thought
- a distinct intuition or strong impression
- the noise of our mind subsides, and a particularly clear thought surfaces which we do not initiate
- a flash of knowledge
- a premonition or "holy hunch"
- a mental picture or visual image of a particular word written on a person
- a dream or mental vision we sense is from God
- on the negative side, a check or hesitancy in our spirit

Each of these inclinations will need to be submitted to the Holy Spirit and God's Word, while being discerned and processed in our own spirits. Acknowledge a lack of peace, or any confusion as a clear indication not to proceed any further.

Simply stated—when in doubt, don't!

---

[28] Psalm 66:18
[29] James 1:8, NKJV
[30] Colossians 3:15a

We must likewise be willing to obey God and flow with His Spirit as He directs us. No leading is too small and insignificant, if it is indeed God speaking.[31]

Like Moses' staff, what appears to be mundane in our own hands may, when yielded to God, emerge as a miracle from Heaven.[32]

SPIRITUAL METEOROLOGISTS

God's people should never be the last ones to figure out what is going on, or what is about to happen. We should live on the tip of the arrow, not somewhere back in the feathers. Scripture makes this quite clear. "When the ram's horn blows a warning, shouldn't the people be alarmed? Does disaster come to a city unless the LORD has planned it? Indeed, the Sovereign LORD never does anything until He reveals His plans to His servants the prophets."[33]

We should live on the tip of the arrow, not somewhere back in the feathers.

God has always had His intuitive forerunners: those tapped into the Spirit of God with a prophetic awareness sent by God. The Book of Chronicles in the Old Testament mentions just such a group. "From the tribe of Issachar, there were 200 leaders of the tribe with their relatives. All these men understood the signs of the times and knew the best course for Israel to take."[34]

Even within the secular culture, the word "initiative" can mean "the aptitude to introduce energy and change, overcoming static inertia in order to act first."

---

31 Zechariah 4:10

32 Exodus 4:1–4

33 Amos 3:6–7

34 1Chronicles 12:32

Jesus severely chided the so-called spiritual leaders of His day, the Pharisees and Sadducees, when they came to test Him. He said, "You know how to interpret the weather signs in the sky, but you don't know how to interpret the signs of the times!"[35] Apparently, Jesus believed spiritual intuition was a prerequisite for every genuine leader of God's people.

But we cannot lead effectively and live in hypocrisy. Though in many corners of the earth, hypocrisy is rampant. For example, according to figures from the World Health Organization, 61 percent of male doctors in China, smoke.[36]

If we discern it, we need to live it. We may not be the first kid on the block to figure out what God is saying, but we need to identify and embrace the truth when we see it (as it is revealed); exposing lies before they have a malignant impact.

Everett M. Rogers' *Innovation Adoption Curve*, which pertains to technological innovations, estimates that:

- 2.5% of people are Innovators
- 13.5% are Early Adopters,
- 68% form the Early and Late Majority
- 16% are Skeptics or Slowpokes

Only God knows what the spiritual counterpart of this principle should be within the church. Eight times in the Gospels Jesus said, "He who has ears to hear, let him hear…"[37] It is my hope and prayer that we who have our ear to the heart of God will be the first to recognize shifts in God's Spirit, the Church and the culture. Only then can we take the initiative to be true leaders, cast in the image and likeness of our Lord and Savior.

---

35 Matthew 16:3b

36 Norris S. The Information-Male Doctors Who Smoke. Financial Times. October 25, 2008. Available at http://www.ft.com/cms/s/0/82de0d64-a22e-11dd-a32f-000077b07658.html?nclick_check=1. Last accessed July 15, 2009.

37 Matthew 11:15, 13:9,13:43, Mark 4:9, 4:23, 7:16, Luke 8:8, 14:35

FRIVOLOUS FORECASTERS

Whole armies of false prophets are about to enter the battle.

Jesus warns, "Beware of false prophets who come disguised as harmless sheep but are really vicious wolves. You can identify them by their fruit, that is, by the way they act. Can you pick grapes from thorn bushes, or figs from thistles?"[38]

There will be no shortage of false prophets in the days ahead. But as Jesus said so clearly, "We will know them by their fruit." John the Apostle likewise warned, "Little children, let no one deceive you. He who practices righteousness is righteous, just as He is righteous."[39]

Obviously, if we lower our own standard of right and wrong, we will soon lack the necessary discernment when we are assaulted by more subtle enticements. Many a well-meaning Christian has left the truth, having mistakenly believed he could dodge deception by entertaining a half-truth. The Apostle Peter, who denied Jesus after He was arrested, knew first-hand how crafty and subtle the enemy of our soul can be. He forewarned all who would come after him, "Stay alert! Watch out for your great enemy, the devil. He prowls around like a roaring lion, looking for someone to devour."[40]

Likewise, Paul dealt with many Christians that would gradually become ensnared by the enemy of their souls. He passionately addressed some legalistic believers in the church at Galatia, "I am shocked that you are turning away so soon from God, who called you to Himself through the loving mercy of Christ. You are following a different way that pretends to be the Good News but is not the Good News at all. You are being fooled by those who deliberately twist the truth concerning Christ."[41]

---

[38] Matthew 7:15–16

[39] 1John 3:7

[40] 1Peter 5:8

[41] Galatians 1:6–7

We too will soon meet a cadre of deceivers, deluding the hearts and minds of men in our own day. The Discerning Church will be vigilant to keep her spiritual antennae's attune to what God considers true. May we preserve the integrity of our relationship with Jesus, so that we can finish our days faithfully following Him. Our lives and the lives of those we love depend on it.

DECEIVED OR DISCERNING

At one time I was profoundly deceived, having fully given myself over to naïve self-indulgence that nearly took my life. The potential to be drawn back to the dark side of life is ever before me. My need for a Savior has never subsided and never will. My only hope is a daily dependence upon my faithful Creator. "…I know the One in whom I trust, and I am sure that He is able to guard what I have entrusted to Him until the day of His return."[42]

Yet, the dangers of Earth surround me. I must therefore be discerning so that I will not squander the priceless inheritance given me.

On April 14, 1999, I had a profound dream. When I woke up, I immediately knew it was from the Lord. Through it, God exposed the depth of sin in my life. After lying in bed and praying for a while, under tremendous conviction, I got up and recorded my dream:

> *Last night I had a dream. I had left my home in the middle of the night and went to the house of another woman. It wasn't really a house. It was more like a bunkhouse— dark, dirty, with a dozen or more bunk beds. In some of the beds were her children. She had no husband. The woman was utterly unattractive, deranged, and dirty. I knew she was dangerous, but still I went to see her. On*

---

[42] 2 Timothy 1:12

the surface, I was going to help her. Underneath was lust.

Soon after arriving in this shady, dingy place, the woman reached out and gave me a long sensuous hug. I did not resist. After a few seconds without saying a word, I climbed into one of the top bunk beds to wait for her. Everything was filthy, but I stayed—waiting—longing for her to come and join me.

All of a sudden, the room began to get very busy. People started to knock on the door. Some of the children in the beds began to make noise. The woman became completely preoccupied. I was waiting in the bed for her to come to me. I was frustrated. "Why won't she come?" I thought. "If we don't get this over with, someone I know is going to find me here. My sin will be exposed. I will be ruined. I will no longer be able to be a pastor."

I felt so vulnerable. My life was now out of my control. I had made my bed. Suddenly, people I knew began to come into the house. I hid under the covers. The room was buzzing with activity. More and more light began to flood the room. "Oh no, they're going to find me!" There was nowhere to hide. I knew these people. They went to my church. Talking to her, and pulling on my covers, they said, "And whom do you have up here?" I resisted their attempts to pull the covers off. Finally they won. I was exposed. When they saw that I was their pastor, their faces were so perplexed and troubled. They asked, "What are you doing here?" "Nothing!" I said, "Nothing happened! Really!" But no plea was able to cover my sin. I had no reasonable explanation, because there was none.

One by one, they began to leave the room, shaking their heads. I was overwhelmed with embarrassment. My heart had been exposed. As I looked over at the woman, she had a subtle smile on her face. She had never intended on fulfilling me, only destroying me.

I woke up and immediately knew the dream was from the Lord. God was exposing the depth of sin in my life. He was showing me my desperate need to not only discern right from wrong, but to act on it. He wanted me to share it with our church family that others might be convicted as well.

Our choices have eternal consequences. Revival is running toward the light and away from darkness, away from the seductive deceptions of Earth to the liberating truth of Heaven. Choose wisely.

FIGHTING THE FOG

The poor choices that so many of us make at times are merely the external behaviors of an inner deception. This struggle in itself is the best indication of a spiritual tug-of-war between our soul's sinful nature and our spirit's longing to become like God.

Paul the apostle describes it best in the Book of Galatians. "So I say, let the Holy Spirit guide your lives. Then you won't be doing what your sinful nature craves. The sinful nature wants to do evil, which is just the opposite of what the Spirit wants. And the Spirit gives us desires that are the opposite of what the sinful nature desires. These two forces are constantly fighting each other, so you are not free to carry out your good intentions."[43]

We grapple to find our true identity in a world that easily succumbs to its sinful nature, falling into the abyss of moral depravity and spiritual deceit. It is to this battlefield that Jesus came. Combining both dimensions in one God-man, He rejected the lures of Earth for the promises of Heaven. Jesus conquered sin and death so that we can, by His Spirit, discern what is true and what is not, what is good and from Heaven, and what is evil and from Hell.

When we realize what He did, it is impossible to not be in-

---

43 Galatians 5:16–17

spired by His life, death, and resurrection. Jesus triumphed over every obstacle, becoming the King over every temptation, lie, and evil so that we could fulfill our purpose as well. It is our destiny!

Upon leaving this Earth, Jesus sent the Comforter, the Holy Spirit of promise, to continue to guide all of His followers. He even empowered them to overcome all that attempted, but failed, to destroy Him. The God of hope has given us that same power, if we would but yield to His will and not our own.

AIDS TO DISCERNMENT

There are protective measures that we can take to shield our hearts so that we are not deceived and led astray from God's best for our lives. "Guard your heart above all else, for it determines the course of your life."[44]

We have already discussed two essential safeguards:
1) allowing God's Spirit to lead and direct our lives, and
2) making sure that what we believe aligns with God's Word, the Bible.

Jesus affirmed these two essential checks and balances when He said, "But the time is coming—indeed it is here now—when true worshipers will worship the Father in spirit and in truth. The Father is looking for those who will worship Him that way."[45]

Another hedge of protection God has provided is accountability. People often confuse appropriate accountability with control.

Control is deciding for others what they can and can not do. Accountability is to account for what others have already done.

---

[44] Proverbs 4:23

[45] John 4:23

> **Control can easily become a power issue, whereas, accountability is designed to be a matter of integrity.**

Control can easily become a power issue, whereas, accountability is designed to be a matter of integrity.

Each of us need people around us who can speak into our lives; to pray for us; to hold our feet to the fire; to provoke us to live in truth— to overcome evil; and to do the right thing.

The great preacher, Charles Spurgeon said, "An unguarded strength is a double weakness." Are we open to be challenged by those who, with no desire to be critical, have our best interest in mind? We don't need just "Yes" men and women around us. We need some "No" folks as well. They too are our real friends. As the scripture says, "…reproofs (correction, reasoning, rebuke) of instruction are the way of life…"[46] Those who win in life are those who are willing to receive correction, even from strangers, the un-churched and those less spiritually mature than we are.

"Wounds from a sincere friend are better than many kisses from an enemy."[47]

Who wouldn't prefer kisses to wounds? But sometimes we need wounds from friends or even enemies, rather than kisses from so-called "friends." I've known lots of people who thought they were safe, just prior to being picked off.

At one point Paul wrote, "Luke, the beloved doctor, sends his greetings, and so does Demas."[48] Some time later he added, "…Demas has forsaken me, having loved this present world, and has departed."[49]

---

[46] Proverbs 6:23b, NKJV (emphasis mine.)

[47] Proverbs 27:6

[48] Colossians 4:14

[49] 2Timothy 4:10, NKJV

When we are too blinded or confused to discern truth, God has a safeguard in His body of believers. Embracing accountability and the uncomfortable death to self will protect us from even the worst consequences.

One of the saddest phone calls I ever heard of took place when a six year old answered the phone. The caller asked, "Can I please speak with your dad?" The young boy replied, "My daddy doesn't live here anymore!"

I don't want to have to explain to someone's child why his daddy is gone!

Nor do I ever want to face my own children, having to tell them I was living a double life.

Deception will launch this level of pain!

Discernment will prevent it!

Prevention is always better than cure.

TEARS OF THE DECEIVED AND DISCERNING

Since the beginning of time, deception has broken the hearts of those who care as God cares.

At one point, deception caused a seemingly insurmountable breach between twin brothers, Jacob and Esau. Eventually, having gone through enough to temper their anger, they embraced, kissed, and wept.[50]

The patriarch Joseph discerned God's gracious heart for his siblings. He "…was overcome with emotion for his brother. He went into his private room, where he broke down and wept."[51]

---

50 Genesis 33:4b

51 Genesis 43:30b

Deception, on the other hand, had caused his brothers to betray him and sell him into slavery. Now it would keep them from believing their transformed brother could completely forgive them for their crime.

In the Old Testament, Joab, the head of David's army, sent a woman to deceive David. Pretending to be in mourning she flattered the king by saying, "…I know that you are like an angel of God in discerning good from evil."[52]

This statement was more accurate than she presently knew. But, much to her surprise, King David discerned that she was lying and that her crocodile tears were not from grief.

But David's clarity of mind would be short-lived. Immediately afterward, when the king met with Joab, he acquiesced to his general's request and allowed his rebellious, unrepentant son, Absalom, to return home. It was a mistake that would cost many lives and place David's entire kingdom in utter peril.

Here is the challenge of discernment. At one moment, we are at the top of our game, identifying truth and lies, good and evil. Later, under the influence of weakness and emotionalism, we let down our guard and allow the enemy a costly foothold.

In the end, Absalom was killed, and his father was heartbroken.

Perhaps his son's untimely death could have been avoided if David had left him in exile until he had a change of heart. Even if true repentance had never occurred, at least Absalom wouldn't have become a threat to David and his people.

Lying tears represent the character of Hell.

Loving tears flow from the heart of Heaven.

---

[52] 2Samuel 14:17

Paul the Apostle was genuinely broken when he wrote, "Dear brothers and sisters, pattern your lives after mine, and learn from those who follow our example. For I have told you often before, and I say it again with tears in my eyes, that there are many whose conduct shows they are really enemies of the cross of Christ. They are headed for destruction. Their god is their appetite, they brag about shameful things, and they think only about this life here on earth."[53]

God's passionate call to obedience continually alerts us to the urgency of the hour, for He alone knows what lies ahead.

Years ago, I had spent extensive time trying to persuade a drug addict to surrender his heart to Jesus. Though his wife was open and prayed, he refused. I continued to pray and reach out to him. He came to church but remained shut down.

One day, I was recording a scripture-based song recounting how Jesus wept over Jerusalem for resisting God's loving hand. I was struggling capturing the appropriate emotion for the extraordinary lyrics when the engineer interrupted, saying I had an urgent phone call. The drug addict I had been ministering to, whose last name was spelled "Christ" had just been shot and killed robbing a Kentucky Fried Chicken. How much did he steal?—Fifteen dollars and change.

After breaking down and weeping for this tragic loss of life, I recorded the song on the very next take.

Discern the hour.

Weep for souls.

---

[53] Philippians 3:17–19

THE DEATH OF PREDICTABLE LIFE

Welcome to the Age of the Unpredictable. The End Times will bring about such unprecedented change at a rate never seen before. Unless we are in tune with God's Spirit, we will not react in time to land on our feet.

Therefore, the last thought we need right now is "I don't need to step up, I'll do it later." The inspiration for this idea comes from the enemy of our soul, who is not omniscient and knows far more about his own future than he does about ours.

Scripture assures us, "...your real life is hidden with Christ in God."[54] Therefore, we must daily follow Jesus in order to live the real life He intended for us and refuse to follow the doomed destiny of some embittered has-been.

"For no one can lay any foundation other than the one we already have—Jesus Christ."[55] Jesus, the Light of the world, is returning, and only clear eyes will see Him.[56]

We all tend to gravitate to the old and familiar: from meals in restaurants to seats in church services. Old shoes tend to feel better. But how do we respond to new menus, new buildings, and new experiences? Either we willingly make new memories or we watch endless reruns of the old. Fossils stay in the same place for a very long time.

So how do we escape this antiquated time warp of predictable life?

We need what is fresh and alive.

My older brother Victor tells the story of buying a fast-food hamburger for one of his grandchildren. Months later, he happened to find it, uneaten, in some obscure portion of his back

---

[54] Colossians 3:3b

[55] 1Corinthians 3:11

[56] Luke 11:34

yard. After all of that time it still looked the same. Nothing had changed. No insects had even disturbed it. Why? Because it wasn't food! So many preservatives had been added that what was left was shelf life, but no actual life.

Christian shelf-life often looks the same everyday. Every church service, even every thought has been so processed, is so predictable, that it no longer has life. Not just for us, but for those around us. Shoppers don't want what we have either, even if it were free! It has become worthless because we have chosen the convenience of pre-packaged thought, rather than organic meals, freshly baked from the ovens of Heaven.

Today, reshuffle the deck.

Let your hair down.

Live!

Blast out of the antiquated time warp of religiosity and into the timeless, spontaneity of the living God.

THE AGE OF URGENCY

A doctor was once on a vacation cruise with his family. It was time for some much needed rest. Early one morning, as he was walking along the deck of the ship, he saw a crowd gathering ahead of him. Bewildered, he asked one of the ship's attendants what had happened. He was told that a passenger had fallen overboard, but that he had been rescued and was undergoing resuscitation.

For a moment, the physician thought about lending a hand, but then decided to let others handle it. He was, of course, on vacation. As he casually passed by he happened to glance over. To his shock he could see that it was his own son who had fallen overboard. The doctor's son was the lifeless person being revived. All of his detached indifference instantly evaporated. This now grief-stricken father aggressively pushed his way through the crowd. His interest had risen to match the need.

Today, someone's son is in trouble. Who will help him?

Right now, a daughter is in desperate need. Who will reach out to her?

What would please the heart of God most?

"…don't forget to do good and to share with those in need. These are the sacrifices that please God."[57]

There is a time to receive and a time to give. Discern the season. God's supply is vast. His help is ready. But sometimes we have to give away what we think we need in order to get what only God knows we truly need.

"Right now you have plenty and can help those who are in need. Later, they will have plenty and can share with you when you need it. In this way, things will be equal."[58]

Perhaps you are the person who is in trouble. Will you humble yourself and ask for help?

God's passionate call to obedience continually alerts us to the urgency of the hour, for He alone knows what lies ahead. Only God's Spirit can communicate to our spirit the appropriate response for every situation.

The Discerning Church will not casually walk by and miss why it was created.

---

[57] Hebrews 13:16

[58] 2Corinthians 8:14

QUESTIONS FOR DISCUSSION

1. Have you ever been part of a church that was deceived? If so, how did that affect your life and the life of your church family?

2. What experience did you have that made you believe your church and/or its leaders were deceived? If so, how has that affected you? If not, are you willing to forgive them now?

3. Have you ever been deceived? If so, what was the issue? How did this deception affect your life and the lives of others around you?

4. What level of discernment do you presently have? How does this level of discernment affect you?

5. What steps can you take to increase discernment in your life? How do you think an increase of spiritual discernment will affect your life and those around you?

6 SUPERNATURAL CHURCH

CHAPTER SIX

"I tell you the truth, anyone who has faith in Me will do what I have been doing. He will do even greater things than these, because I am going to the Father."

JESUS[1]

THE SUPERNATURAL GOSPEL

When the prophet Elijah faced off with the 450 prophets of Baal on Mount Carmel, it was the mother-of-all power encounters. He asked the people of Israel to choose between the demon-god Baal, and the living God of Heaven.

It would seem to be a simple choice. Tragically, they remained silent, not answering him.

Elijah then challenged the fully demonized prophets to send down fire to burn their sacrifice. Though there is no shortage of fire in Hell, after dancing and cutting themselves, these false prophets could not even muster a single flame. Elijah, on the other hand, called down fire from Heaven to consume the sacrifice on a water-soaked altar.[2]

Why don't we see this type of collision between good and evil in our day?

---

1 John 14:12

2 1Kings 18:20–40

The price of admission into this supernatural lifestyle requires complete surrender of our will, and total obedience to the purpose of God.

Are we separated from God's supernatural hand by various sins that limit His ability to move on our behalf? Do fear, unbelief, doubt, and other impurities contaminate the flow of God's anointed power through us? "The LORD's arm is not too weak to save you, nor is His ear too deaf to hear you call. It's your sins that have cut you off from God. Because of your sins, He has turned away and will not listen anymore."[3]

Nehemiah himself describes the pitiful condition of his beloved city Jerusalem. "The survivors who are left from the captivity in the province are there in great distress and reproach. The wall of Jerusalem is also broken down, and its gates are burned with fire." In response he "sat down and wept, and mourned for many days." He also "was fasting and praying before the God of heaven."[4]

Nehemiah took personal responsibility for the sins and poor judgments of his ancestors. These verses perfectly describe the pressing need in this critical hour: "God help us! Bring us together in prayer and fasting, so that we may entreat you to move Heaven and Earth."

Many of us readily accept that Jesus performed miracles and healed people while He was on this Earth.[5] But do we likewise believe that Jesus, through the power of the Holy Spirit, longs to perform miracles and heal people today?[6]

If we do, then we should believe that He wants His Spirit to flow through us in order to see others healed: spirit, soul and body. Jesus pledged, "I tell you the truth, anyone who believes

---

[3] Isaiah 59:1–2

[4] Nehemiah 1:3–4

[5] Luke 7:11–16, Matthew 9:18–19, 23–26, Mark 5:22–24, 35–43; Luke 8:41–42, 49–56, John 11:14; 12:9

[6] Acts 2:43, 4:16, 5:12, 14:3; Romans 15:19; 2Corinthians 12:12; Mark 16:18; Luke 10:19; Acts 28:3–6, 5:15, 19:11–12, 9:36–40, 20:9–12

in Me will do the same works I have done, and even greater (larger) works, because I am going to be with the Father."[7]

As He commissioned the early disciples, so He has appointed us. "Jesus called His twelve disciples together and gave them authority to cast out evil spirits and to heal every kind of disease and illness,"[8] saying, "Heal the sick, raise the dead, cure those with leprosy, and cast out demons. Give as freely as you have received!"[9]

He has promised, "'These miraculous signs will accompany those who believe: They will cast out demons in My name, and they will speak in new languages. They will be able to handle snakes with safety, and if they drink anything poisonous, it won't hurt them. They will be able to place their hands on the sick, and they will be healed.' And the disciples went everywhere and preached, and the Lord worked through them, confirming what they said by many miraculous signs."[10]

In order for the Kingdom of Heaven to infiltrate Earth and the Church to rise in her full, supernatural anointing, the King of Kings must be established in our midst. God must lead.

His presence must be our centerpiece.

His prayer must motivate us.

His power must propel us.

Today, and in the years to come, as we allow God's Spirit to fill and overflow our inner lives, we will see the greater works Jesus promised. Yet, the price of admission into this supernatural lifestyle requires complete surrender of our will, and total obedience to the purpose of God.[11]

---

7 John 14:12
8 Matthew 10:1
9 Matthew 10:8
10 Mark 16:17–18, 20
11 Isaiah 1:19, Philippians 2:8, Revelation 2:10

A supernatural lifestyle is not only possible.

It is God's will for each of us.

LEADING GOD

One Sunday, after speaking at a weekend church service, the extraordinary presence of God led our church into an extended time of worship. Though we would normally have ended this last weekend service at a particular time, God's anointing was so tangible it would have been jarring to break away.

During the additional hour of worship, the atmosphere was so thick with the life of God that I lay prostrate on my face and just wept. While in His presence God spoke to my spirit, His words convict me to this day.

God said very clearly, "I don't want to be led!"

We are so conditioned in our service to God, we lead out of habit instead of following out of obedience.

He was gentle, but crystal clear, and very firm. Obviously, the Lord wouldn't have said this to me if I were not in some way hindering Him from fully leading.

Now you know why I was crying.

As you might imagine, it has never been one of my goals to lead God.

Consequently, I was broken hearted at the thought that this was exactly what I was doing. For a dozen "good" reasons I can attempt to move ahead of God and miss out on all of the "great" He intends for my life and for our church family.

This is a common dilemma for many Christians and leaders, but not one that we would perhaps want to admit. We are so conditioned in our service to God, we lead out of habit instead of following out of obedience.

During the next series of weekend services I repented before our church family in the hopes that this public acknowledgement would provoke me to be more sensitive to the slightest promptings of God's Spirit.

"For all who are led (guided and directed) by the Spirit of God are children of God."[12] We are not made children of God by being led by His Spirit. However, an indicator of a proper relationship with Him is allowing His Spirit to lead.

Knowing God will always come down to flowing with God.

"On the last day, that great day of the feast, Jesus stood and cried out, saying, 'If anyone thirsts, let him come to Me and drink. He who believes in Me, as the Scripture has said, out of his heart will flow rivers of living water.' But this He spoke concerning the Spirit, whom those believing in Him would receive…"[13]

God wants to flow in us and through us.

The words of C.S. Lewis provide a chilling exhortation, "There are two kinds of people: those who say to God, 'Thy will be done,' and those to whom God says, 'All right, then, have it your way.'"[14] Becoming the latter would destroy our future. We must not be seduced into pampering our present.

May God keep us from becoming those Jesus spoke of in the Book of Matthew, "These people honor Me with their lips, but their hearts are far from Me."[15]

The Supernatural Church must let God lead.

Only He knows where we are going.

---

12 Romans 8:14

13 John 7:37–39a, NKJV

14 Lewis CS. *The Great Divorce* (1945).

15 Matthew 15:8

FAST-TRACK FAITH

In 1973, my twin brother Joseph was still fully immersed in Eastern religions and living in India and Nepal for a year and a half. While he was overseas, our two sisters and one brother had given their hearts to Jesus. We were all particularly concerned for Joseph, having not heard any word from him in over six months. My brother-in-law, George, who had experienced a dramatic conversion, was so unsettled about Joseph's well-being that he went on a seven day fast.

> **God is going to use fasting and prayer as a major weapon in the battle for the hearts and minds of men.**

We didn't realize the impact of these seven days of prayer and fasting until some time later. Their affect was nothing short of miraculous. During the exact days George was interceding for Joseph, Joseph was in Delhi, India. While in his room meditating, a cross of light illuminated on the door and God spoke to his spirit, "Jesus is the way."[16]

It was divine intervention!

At the time, Joseph was experiencing a number of meta-physical phenomena, and so this event did not cause him to surrender his heart to Jesus. But it certainly served as a catalyst to point him in the direction of his sisters' and brother's newfound faith in Jesus Christ.

Within a few weeks he was back in the United States and a short time later he surrendered his life to Jesus. Since 1983, he has directed *Forward Edge*, a Christian relief and mission's organization that sends hundreds of teams around the world to share Christ's love with those affected by poverty, disaster and sickness.

---

16 John 14:6

In the years to come, God is going to use fasting and prayer as a major weapon in the battle for the hearts and minds of men. The Supernatural Church will arise as she humbles herself. A new generation of whole-hearted disciples will rise to accurately access the critical need of the hour, overcoming evil with good through prayer and fasting. Paul wrote, "I have worked hard and long, enduring many sleepless nights. I have been hungry and thirsty and have often gone without food."[17]

Those burdened by God to intercede for others will get up early, stay up late, fast from food and fun in order to fulfill the call on their lives.

One day, someone who periodically attended our church approached me. I knew his two-year old daughter was about to undergo an operation and so I was eager to pray with him for her. He could sense my concern for his daughter and appreciated my offer to pray. But, he said, "I need something further." He told me, "My daughter goes in for surgery very early Monday morning. Could you have your entire staff come to my home and pray for her before she goes to the hospital?" He suggested 4:30 in the morning.

What struck me was not that a father would be so eager to receive help for his daughter. I can completely understand that. What startled me was that his overwhelming burden would cause him to make such an outrageous request without hesitation. He was not tentative to appeal for help because he viewed the need to be so great.

In one sense, this desperate dad perfectly modeled the heart of an intercessor. Those burdened by God to intercede for others will get up early, stay up late, fast from food and fun in order to fulfill the call on their lives. Their God-given sense of urgency is so real, so pressing, that what would be considered outrageous to others is the staple of life for them.

Welcome to the life of an End Time intercessor.

---

[17] 2Corinthians 11:27a

We will see a significant increase in followers of Jesus willing to fast and pray for individuals and nations to come to a saving relationship with Jesus. As He Himself said, "My food is to do the will of Him who sent Me, and to finish His work."[18]

THE "NEAR AUDIBLE" VOICE OF GOD

In mid-August 1999, our dear friends, John and Patty from Missouri, visited my wife Suzie and me. We spent one long evening discussing the newly founded worship and prayer ministry of the International House of Prayer (IHOP). It had just been launched in Kansas City the previous May. IHOP would not begin its present 24–7 dimension of worship and prayer until September of that year.

In the middle of the night, after our conversation about IHOP, God woke me with a vision. I got up at 2 a.m., wrote it down, and sent it to IHOP's Director, Mike Bickle. Here is that vision:

> *As I lay in bed tonight in semi-sleep, snapshots came across my thoughts. In my mind's eye I saw a dark sea of faceless figures (not a sea of dark figures). None were identifiable and for a while I didn't know what they were. The figures were crammed together, millions upon millions of them. Periodically, there would be a flash of light and a singular image could be seen passing over them. It was not, however, readily identifiable. Though this scene repeated itself over and over again, I did not recognize the object. Even when it was illuminated, it was indistinguishable—not just to me, but seemingly to all.*
>
> *During these momentary flashes, there would be a great stirring throughout the sea. As this scene repeatedly occurred, I could see the singular object was a flag,*

---

18 John 4:34

a banner; I sensed it was important. The sea of figures were human spirits representing the Body of Christ.

The banner became visible when there was an attempt to raise it. It was as if light from some invisible source would illuminate it. Most of the time, the flag seemed to be lifted almost by accident. But then there began to be a concerted effort to lift it. With each attempt, the sea became more agitated, affecting everyone. Eventually, I could see threads flowing from the banner and attaching themselves to all in the sea. It now appeared that if this flag could be held upright, light would remain on it.

Worship was revealed as the common thread. All true Christians felt its tug. But in its periodic state, it represented more of Earth's timeframe than Heaven's. If its constant pulse could be sustained, immense light would overpower the darkness. However, most did not realize the value of the banner until it was fully upright. And the price for raising it was enormous. Consequently, attempts to hoist it failed.

Worship…if its constant pulse could be sustained, immense light would overpower the darkness.

I had no idea at that time that the International House of Prayer[19] would so affectively open doors to 24–7 worship and intercession. It was beyond my understanding that this burgeoning prayer movement would circle the globe and touch millions of lives and that our own church would host a House of Prayer beginning in August 2004.

---

19 www.ihop.org

THE CHURCH AS A HOUSE OF PRAYER

Near the end of Christ's earthly ministry He wept over Jerusalem because its inhabitants didn't know the way of peace God had chosen for them. He was broken-hearted that they would soon be destroyed, and their children with them. This was primarily because they didn't know their time of visitation—their hour of divine opportunity.[20]

It is not a coincidence that in the very next verse Jesus drove out the thieves in the temple who were robbing God and His people. Later in the Gospel of John Jesus affirmed, "the thief's purpose is to steal and kill and destroy. My purpose is to give them a rich and satisfying life."[21]

So what did Jesus lament most while weeping over the eminent captivity of His beloved people, and after driving the thieves from His temple? He announced, "The Scriptures declare, 'My Temple will be a house of prayer,' but you have turned it into a den of thieves."[22]

Christ's church, as a house of prayer, along with His saturating presence, will be fulfilled in these Last Days.

Christ's church, as a house of prayer, along with His saturating presence, will be fulfilled in these Last Days, both individually and corporately, prior to the return of Jesus.[23]

58 percent of Americans say they pray every day. An additional 17 percent do so weekly. That means 75 percent of Americans pray at some point during each week. Only 7 percent say they have never prayed.[24] 24 percent of Americans are now atheists, agnostics, or deists.[25]

---

20 Luke 19:41-44

21 John 10:10

22 Luke 19:46

23 Isaiah 56:7, Matthew 21:13, Mark 11:17

24 Pew Forum on Religion & Public Life survey based on interviews with more than 35,000 Americans ages 18 and older. Published June 23, 2008.

25 American Religious Identification Survey, Conducted between February and November of 2008

In the midst of this somewhat-prayerful American culture, a 24-hour worship and prayer movement is rising to encircle the globe.

Though it will emerge in many diverse structures and forms, Jesus' prayer to the Father will be fulfilled: "May Your Kingdom come soon. May Your will be done on Earth, as it is in Heaven."[26] The tenor of Heaven is filled even now through worship and prayer and soon this all-encompassing dimension in Heaven is coming to Earth!

> **Without God's tangible presence permeating our lives, we are a mere shell of our potential—clouds without rain, wells without water.**

The centerpiece of our relationship with God has always been about His presence. From the Garden of Eden[27] to Moses' tabernacle,[28] from Solomon's Temple[29] to eternity in Heaven,[30] God longs to be with us and us with Him, now and forever.

Without God's tangible presence permeating our lives, we are a mere shell of our potential—clouds without rain, wells without water. But this longing for intimate relationship cannot just persist in His heart alone, it must be birthed in ours as well.

When the Children of Israel were in the wilderness, Moses built a tabernacle to the Lord—the forerunner of David's Temple, built by his son Solomon.

The Book of Exodus recounts the story:

> *"It was Moses' practice to take the Tent of Meeting and set it up some distance from the camp. Everyone who wanted to make a request of the LORD would go to the Tent of Meeting outside the camp. Whenever Moses went out to the Tent of Meeting, all the people would get*

---

26 Matthew 6:10
27 Genesis 3:8
28 Exodus 29:42
29 2Chronicles 5:11–14
30 Revelation 21 and 22

> *up and stand in the entrances of their own tents. They would all watch Moses until he disappeared inside. As he went into the tent, the pillar of cloud would come down and hover at its entrance while the LORD spoke with Moses. When the people saw the cloud standing at the entrance of the tent, they would stand and bow down in front of their own tents. Inside the Tent of Meeting, the LORD would speak to Moses face to face, as one speaks to a friend. Afterward Moses would return to the camp, but the young man who assisted him, Joshua son of Nun, would remain behind in the Tent of Meeting."*[31]

At that time, communion with God took place vicariously through one person: Moses. But God intends an intimate relationship with all of His sons and daughters.

"Then Moses said, 'If you don't personally go with us, don't make us leave this place. How will anyone know that You look favorably on me—on me and on Your people—if You don't go with us? For Your presence among us sets Your people and me apart from all other people on the earth.'"[32]

God's desire has always been that: "I will walk among you; I will be your God, and you will be My people."[33] Through constant assault from the Garden of Eden until this day, relationship remains our Creator's highest priority.

King David, a man who desperately wanted to fulfill God's purposes,[34] brought the Ark of the Covenant, the focal point of Moses' Tabernacle, to be the centerpiece of God's Temple in Jerusalem.[35] There, David gathered all that was necessary to build a Temple for God on Earth.[36]

---

[31] Exodus 33:7–11

[32] Exodus 33:15–16

[33] Leviticus 26:12

[34] 1Samuel 13:14, Acts 13:22

[35] 1Chronicles 15, 2Chronicles 1:4

[36] 1Chronicles chapters 22, 28 and 29

Later, at the dedication of David's Temple by his son Solomon, the presence of God was so tangible that the priests could not stand and minister:

> *"The trumpeters and singers performed together in unison to praise and give thanks to the LORD. Accompanied by trumpets, cymbals, and other instruments, they raised their voices and praised the LORD with these words: 'He is good! His faithful love endures forever!' At that moment a thick cloud filled the Temple of the LORD. The priests could not continue their service because of the cloud, for the glorious presence of the LORD filled the Temple of God."*[37]

God's plan has always been to raise up a kingdom of priests to minister to Him and for Him prior to His return.[38] The final generation will take this holy commission seriously and make ready a resting place for God's presence to dwell on Earth.

This is truly supernatural!

SIGNS FROM HEAVEN

Miraculous impartations and visitations are coming to Earth. They're giving us a glimpse through supernatural portals into Heaven. In eternity, all who have been resurrected to live with God forever in Heaven will have complete understanding, will be fully healed, will be fully known, and will live transparent lives. For now, we struggle to understand, to believe, to be known, to live honest, vulnerable and transparent lives before God and man.

Jesus was the perfect example of this kind of Spirit-led life. The Bible says that, "…God publicly endorsed Jesus the Nazarene by doing powerful miracles, wonders, and signs

---

37 2Chronicles 5:13–14

38 Exodus 19:6, Revelation 1:6, 5:10

This grace to perform supernatural signs and wonders has been extended to all Christ followers.

through Him."[39] He knew that His life, ministry, and miracles would verify that God had indeed sent Him. Jesus said about his teachings and miracles, "The Father gave Me these works to accomplish, and they prove that He sent Me."[40] As Christ's earthly ministry was confirmed with supernatural signs, so is ours. "…God confirmed the message by giving signs, wonders, and gifts of the Holy Spirit whenever He chose."[41]

This grace to perform supernatural signs and wonders has been extended to all Christ followers. It is a significant part of God's miraculous, multiplying strategy. "Jesus called His twelve disciples together and gave them authority to cast out evil spirits and to heal every kind of disease and illness."[42]

You could say His commission was supernormal and extramundane. "Heal the sick, raise the dead, cure those with leprosy, and cast out demons. Give as freely as you have received!"[43]

He said it.

They did it.

We can only give what we have received. So, it is fitting for us to receive all of the healing and miraculous impartation God has for us. Others are waiting to be healed on the other side of our own restoration. "And the disciples went everywhere and preached, and the Lord worked through them, confirming what they said by many miraculous signs."[44]

---

39 Acts 2:22a

40 John 5:36a

41 Hebrews 2:4

42 Matthew 10:1

43 Matthew 10:8

44 Mark 16:20

This call for divine proclamation and empowerment has never been rescinded. Jesus predicted it would effectively encircle and envelope the whole Earth. He promised, "And this gospel of the kingdom will be preached in all the world as a witness (something evidential, with proof, with evidence) to all the nations, and then the end will come."[45]

Jesus was saying that the gospel and our witness should be preached with something to verify its authenticity.

The good news of God's magnificent plan for man centers on what Jesus accomplished by dying on the cross for our sins. "The message of the cross is foolish to those who are headed for destruction! But we who are being saved know it is the very power of God."[46] The word power in this verse is *dunamis*, and is most often translated as "miracles" or "miraculous powers." So, the gospel message itself has the miraculous power to transform.

The Supernatural Church will share it, live it, and see it transform those desperately in need of Jesus.

LYING SIGNS

In contrast to God granting signs and wonders from Heaven, our adversary will simultaneously demonstrate lying signs from Hell.

"…Satan disguises himself as an angel of light. So it is no wonder that his servants also disguise themselves as servants of righteousness."[47]

---

[45] Matthew 24:14, NKJV (emphasis mine.)
[46] 1Corinthians 1:18
[47] 2Corinthians 11:14b–15a

We live in a generation that believes in the supernatural but runs from God.

Prior to Moses' appointment with Pharaoh, God told him to "…take your shepherd's staff with you, and use it to perform the miraculous signs I have shown you."[48] Moses stepped out in faith and God did as He had promised.

But simultaneously, "…Pharaoh called in his own wise men and sorcerers, and these Egyptian magicians did the same thing with their magic."[49]

These magicians, "…Jannes and Jambres opposed Moses… (having) depraved minds and a counterfeit faith."[50]

In April 2000, Newsweek found that 84 percent of Americans polled believe that God performs miracles and 77 percent believe God or the saints cure or heal people given no chance of survival by medical science without medical hope.

By June 2008, 80 percent still believe miracles occur.[51]

We live in a generation that believes in the supernatural but runs from God. This opens the door wide for the enemy to enact his seductive forgeries. Many counterfeit miracles and healings will flood the coming age. It will be a spiritual minefield requiring extraordinary discernment and sensitivity to God's Spirit. "For false messiahs and false prophets will rise up and perform great signs and wonders so as to deceive, if possible, even God's chosen ones."[52]

---

48 Exodus 4:17

49 Exodus 7:11

50 2Timothy 3:8a

51 Pew Forum on Religion & Public Life survey based on interviews with more than 35,000 Americans ages 18 and older. Published June 23, 2008.

52 Matthew 24:24, Mark 13:22. See 2Thessalonians 2:9, Revelation 13:13–14; 16:14; 19:20

Paul the Apostle wrote of the treacherous days prior to the return of Jesus: "…that day will not come until there is a great rebellion against God[53] and the man of lawlessness is revealed—the one who brings destruction."[54]

"This man will come to do the work of Satan with counterfeit power and signs and miracles. So God will cause them to be greatly deceived, and they will believe these lies. Then they will be condemned for enjoying evil rather than believing the truth."[55]

One of the great seductions of the End Times will be lying signs and wonders performed by emissaries of Satan and not servants of God. May God give us the wisdom and discernment to know the difference.

FOOD FIGHT

Adam and Eve plunged the entire human race into sin over food. They succumbed to the lust of the flesh, the lust of the eyes, and the pride of life. "The woman…saw that the tree was beautiful and its fruit looked delicious, and she wanted the wisdom it would give her. So she took some of the fruit and ate it. Then she gave some to her husband, who was with her, and he ate it too."[56] "For all that is in the world—the lust of the flesh, the lust of the eyes, and the pride of life—is not of the Father but is of the world."[57]

---

[53] "the falling away comes first," NKJV

[54] 2Thessalonians 2:3b

[55] 2Thessalonians 2:9, 11–12

[56] Genesis 3:6

[57] 1John 2:16

Jesus, the last Adam,[58] succeeded where the first Adam failed. Three times He was tempted by Satan in the wilderness; first with bread;[59] then with the pride of life;[60] and lastly with the lust of the eyes.[61] He overcame so that we can also.

For many, the battle over food set in motion a chain reaction of obedience or disobedience that had long-term repercussions.

- Jacob's brother Esau sold his birthright for a hot meal.[62]
- The Israelites murmured against God in the wilderness because of food and consequently forfeited His blessing.[63]
- The house of Eli, the high priest, bore a curse because his sons ate part of the offering that belonged to God.[64]
- The infamous city of Sodom was guilty of the sin of "fullness of food".[65]

Likewise, healthy relationships with food and fasting have birthed great moves of God.

- The leaders of the church at Antioch founded a worldwide missions movement in the 1st century as they worshiped the Lord with prayer and fasting.[66]
- During the 2nd and 3rd centuries the early church fasted two days a week.
- Polycarp in 110 A.D., urged fasting among the saints as a powerful aid against temptation and fleshly lusts.
- Tertullian wrote a treatise on the subject in 210 A.D. In it, he defended fasting as a better minister of religion than feasting.

---

58 1Corinthians 15:45
59 Matthew 4:3–4
60 Matthew 4:5–7
61 Matthew 4:8–11
62 Genesis 25:34
63 Numbers 11:4–5, 21:5; Psalm 78:29–31
64 1Samuel 2:12–17
65 Ezekiel 16:49
66 Acts 13

- The great reformer Martin Luther used to fast frequently. He said his flesh would grumble dreadfully at abstinence, but fast he would, for he found that when he was fasting, it quickened his praying. Luther fasted for days while translating the Bible and here undoubtedly lies the secret of his unrivaled translation. Fasting was also responsible for ushering in the great Reformation, which changed the destiny of Europe.

- John Calvin, noted expositor of the Scriptures, was also a man who fasted regularly. He lived to see his prayers answered in the conversion of almost an entire city.

- John Knox fasted and waited upon God in Scotland until intervening Providence drove Mary Queen of Scots into exile.

- The leaders of the Reformation in England practiced fasting as faithfully as they offered their prayers.

- The lives of great Christian leaders: Charles Finney, Jonathan Edwards, John Wesley, Charles Spurgeon, and many others, saw fasting as a major part of their ministries.

- Charles Finney, a man who experienced some of the greatest revivals in history, declared that when he detected a diminishing presence of God's Spirit in him, he would fast for three days and nights. After doing so, he testified of a re-filling of the Holy Spirit's marvelous power."[67]

Fasting and prayer are necessary for the supernatural release of the power of God in our world.

---

[67] Cove C. *Revival Now! Through Prayer and Fasting* (Schmul Publishing Company, 1988).

Fasting can fuel many profound spiritual dimensions:

- Increasing our sensitivity to God's Spirit.[68]
- Humbling us.[69]
- Establishing priorities in our lives.
- Working out areas of imbalance.
- Making us appreciate the many blessings we have been given.
- Showing us what is most important in our lives.
- Bringing our areas of weakness and susceptibility before God.

Fasting and prayer are necessary for the supernatural release of the power of God in our world. Here are some practical tips for fasting.

There are four types of fasts:

1. *Complete Fast*—no food or drink—maximum time: 3 days and 3 nights.[70] Supernaturally Sustained—40 Days and 40 Nights. This is only possible because of a divine enabling.[71]

2. *Normal Fast*—no food, only water. Water may be in the form of plain drinking water, lemon water, herbal tea, etc.

3. *Partial Fast*—Eliminate certain food and drinks.[72]

4. *Group Fast*—corporate fasting as God directs.[73]

---

[68] Ezra 8:21

[69] Psalm 35:13

[70] Ezra 10:6, Esther 4:16, Acts 9:9

[71] Exodus 34:28, Deuteronomy 9:9,18, 1Kings 19:8, Matthew 17:3

[72] Daniel 10:2-3, 1Kings 17, Matthew 3:4

[73] 2Chronicles 20:1–4, Ezra 8:21–23, Joel 1:14

What inhibits Christians from experiencing fasting and its many benefits?

1. Ignorance of the value of fasting.[74]
2. Self-centered lifestyle.[75]
3. Indifference toward the purposes of God.[76]
4. Lack of self-control.[77]
5. Wrong priorities.[78]
6. False concept of Christianity.[79]
7. Insincerity toward the Lordship of Jesus.[80]

FAITHFUL FRUIT, MIGHTY MIRACLES

One of the supernatural stewardships God gives to those who follow Him is being a guardian of the truth. Our relationship with God will always be tested for its integrity. Proverbs says, "The integrity (innocence) of the upright (straightforward) will guide them, but the perversity (twisted distortion) of the unfaithful (disloyal) will destroy (devastate) them."[81]

My heart breaks as I write this verse. Just mentioning the words, *twisted*, *distorted*, *disloyal* and *devastated*, fans the faces of so many that I've seen come and go from the headlines of Christianity over the years. They blew in, blew up and blew out. At times masses followed, only to be tragically disappointed by a leader's lack of integrity, innocence, uprightness and a straightforward walk with Jesus.

---

74 Hosea 4:6

75 Colossians 3:1–3, Romans 12:1

76 Job 23:12

77 Galatians 5:22–23, Mark 8:34–35

78 Matthew 6:33, Romans 14:17

79 2Corinthians 6:4–5, 2Corinthians 11:27

80 Philippians 3:19, Romans 16:18, Proverbs 30:8

81 Proverbs 11:3, NKJV (emphasis mine.)

I'd rather walk in faithful fruit, than see mighty miracles.

Disingenuousness placed a stumbling block in front of those to come, who minister for the Lord in sincerity and truth. As Paul wrote, "For our boasting is this: the testimony of our conscience that we conducted ourselves in the world in simplicity and godly sincerity, not with fleshly wisdom but by the grace of God."[82]

Jesus qualified the inevitable result of a shallow relationship with Him: "A tree is identified by its fruit. If a tree is good, its fruit will be good. If a tree is bad, its fruit will be bad."[83]

He is saying, "My followers will be known by their fruit, not by their gifts."

Paul the Apostle then clarifies exactly the kind of fruit Jesus is talking about. "But the Holy Spirit produces this kind of fruit in our lives: love, joy, peace, patience, kindness, goodness, faithfulness, gentleness, and self-control. There is no law against these things! Those who belong to Christ Jesus have nailed the passions and desires of their sinful nature to His cross and crucified them there. Since we are living by the Spirit, let us follow the Spirit's leading in every part of our lives."[84]

I'd rather walk in faithful fruit, than see mighty miracles.

If I am living a double life, my duplicity will eventually bring a far greater reproach than the sum total of all of the signs or wonders God may ever allow me to walk in. Though I thank God, this is not an either/or option, I must keep my heart unwavering, focused on being pure.[85] Then will I not only see God, but others will see God in me. Only by fixing my "… thoughts on what is true, and honorable, and right, and pure,

---

[82] 2Corinthians 1:12, 2:17, Ephesians 6:24, Titus 2:7

[83] Matthew 12:33

[84] Galatians 5:22-25

[85] Matthew 5:8

and lovely, and admirable,"[86] will I be able to showcase His life to a world aching to behold His face in righteousness.[87]

Jesus said, "…wisdom is shown to be right by its results."[88] What could the devil offer you that would cause you to compromise your character? You had better search it out and deal with it before the enemy of your soul does.

There is never a need to rush, leaving the peace of God for the sake of expediency.

There are no shortcuts in God, only detours.

The Supernatural Church will be like the "wise man who built his house on the rock," because when "the rain descended, the floods came, and the winds blew and beat on that house, it did not fall, for it was founded on the rock."[89]

---

86 Philippians 4:8

87 Psalm 17:15

88 Matthew 11:19

89 Matthew 7:24b–25b, NKJV

QUESTIONS FOR DISCUSSION

1. Have you ever experienced God's Spirit moving supernaturally? How did that experience affect you?

2. Have you personally moved in the supernatural realm to help someone else? What was that like for you and the other person?

3. Do you think flowing in the supernatural realm will become a greater part of your life in the days to come? If so, what supernatural realms has God called you to move in?

4. Have you ever chosen to take the time to fast and pray? What happened during this time? If not, are you willing to fast and pray for something/someone now? If so, for what/who?

5. As you read about the fruit of the Spirit in Galatians 5:22–25: love, joy, peace, patience, kindness, goodness, faithfulness, gentleness, and self-control, what specific fruit do you think the Lord is wanting you to grow in during this season of your life? How do you think that would affect you and others around you?

VIRTUAL CHURCH

CHAPTER SEVEN

"When you are in love you can't fall asleep because reality is better than your dreams."

DR. SEUSS

THE DAWN OF COMMUNICATION

Ever since Adam first whispered to his newly created wife, "Good morning sweetness! Hungry?" a passion to communicate has been foremost on our minds. This insatiable longing to share with others has been passed down from our heavenly Father. He is the Communicator-in-Chief! Even the word communicate comes from the Latin word *communere*, which means, "to share."

Some time prior to Adam's possible first words on Earth, God spoke a declarative sentence, "Let there be light."[1] This same light has been overpowering darkness ever since.

As God is the supreme Author of all that is worth communicating,[2] He is:

- The Truth that sets free, unmasking every lie.[3]
- The Word eternal, that was, is, and always will be.[4]

---

[1] Genesis 1:3

[2] Hebrews 5:9, 12:2

[3] John 8:32, 14:6

[4] John 1:1–2

The Bible describes, in infinite terms, God's essence and passion to communicate.

The Bible describes, in infinite terms, God's essence and passion to communicate: "In the beginning the Word already existed. The Word was with God, and the Word was God. He existed in the beginning with God. God created everything through Him, and nothing was created except through Him. The Word gave life to everything that was created, and His life brought light to everyone. So the Word became human and made His home among us. He was full of unfailing love and faithfulness. And we have seen His glory, the glory of the Father's one and only Son."[5]

Throughout history our God-given need to communicate has progressed dramatically from:

- oral to written
- smoke signals to story telling
- pigeons to pony express
- printing to typewriters, telegraph, telephones and televisions
- radio to satellites, cell phones and search engines
- computers to chat rooms
- internet to email
- broadcasting to broadband
- instant messaging to text messaging

From drums to digital, we've come a long way… but what is ahead will be far more dramatic than what has already transpired.

The gloves limiting communication are coming off.

---

[5] John 1:1–4, 14

7—VIRTUAL CHURCH

The master strategy of God is about to be revealed.

The linchpin in the completion of the Great Commission is being put in place.

INTERNET FEVER

Let me tell you a story.

Once upon a time, when a person wanted to research a subject, or locate a footnote or quote, he would trek down to the local public library and spend hours rummaging through massive card files. In the event he thought he found a book title that might contain pertinent information, he would then search the shelves for the book. If, per chance, he found the volume he wanted, minutes to hours would be spent trying to retrieve the particular details he was hoping to find. In more cases than not, he would leave the library relatively unsuccessful. It was the very definition of frustration.

When was this?

The 70's! No, not the 1870's, the 1970's!

So let me ask you, have you hugged your computer lately?

You have, at your fingertips, access to more information at light-speed than Albert Einstein ever dreamed of.

And there is every indication that use of this marvelous invention called the Internet will only increase.

In Europe, for example, the use of the Internet is even more pervasive. In the United Kingdom, Germany, and France, the Internet has nearly double the influence of television— the second strongest medium, and has almost eight times

> "Research shows that the Internet stands out as the most important communications medium."
>
> —Dave Senay

the influence of print media. TV and print will never recover. This transition is irreversible.[6]

One European executive said, "The research shows that the Internet stands out as the most important communications medium in the lives of European consumers today."[7]

In the U.S., some 55 percent of all adult Americans now have a high-speed Internet connection at home.[8] The percentage of Americans with broadband at home has grown from 47 percent in early 2007.[9]

The availability, quality, cost, and value of Internet services continue to provide an open invitation for a new age band of users. A younger generation avails itself of the instant global universe at its fingertips. What will meet them on the other side of curiosity? Truth that transforms? Or lies that will further block the way from the God they so desperately need?

The question should never be, "Am I interested?" But rather, "What are God's interests for me?" Begin the inquiry. Before life on Earth is finished, each of us will most likely be surprised at the unthinkable stewardships we will be given. Prepare your heart for the unexpected. It is coming sooner than we think.

---

[6] Pew Research Polls Internet

[7] Dave Senay, president and chief executive officer of Fleishman-Hillard

[8] Pew Research Polls Internet, 7/2/2008

[9] Pew Research Polls Internet

GOD IN THE DEAD ROOM

My Italian mother had some unique generational quirks that some of you may find familiar. We had a living room that was almost never used. Thick plastic covered beautifully ornate furniture to protect it from… I don't know. Human beings? Perhaps two over-active twin boys? Whatever the reason, the room was out-of-bounds, especially for anything living. Our affectionate term for it was the *Dead Room*, because the amount of hours my mother allowed us to be in it could be counted on two hands.

One of the dangers facing the church of the future is that it will become the *Dead Room*; a place rarely visited because the stewards of the church fail to see its true value and significance. They clean and preserve for, frankly, the wrong reasons. Proverbs says, "Without oxen a stable stays clean, but you need a strong ox for a large harvest."[10] May God remove the plastic in us that inadvertently keeps others from experiencing genuine living.

True Christians get dirty. They skin their knees. They break some bones and do whatever is necessary to reach the lost.

If we stay in the grandstands we won't get dirty. But this is not what God intended. Only as we venture onto the field, will we move from being passive observers to active participants in the battle for eternal souls. True Christians get dirty. They skin their knees. They break some bones and do whatever is necessary to reach the lost. The Bible clearly states that, "…all of this is a gift from God, who brought us back to Himself through Christ. And God has given us this task of reconciling people to Him."[11]

---

10 Proverbs 14:4

11 2Corinthians 5:18

Reconciling people to God is not the call of a select few, but the universal stewardship given to all true Christians. Our roles, functions and capacities will vary, but Jesus Himself has given us our high and holy calling. He has commissioned each of us, once and for all time to, "Go into all the world and preach the Good News to everyone."[12]

This challenge is still in effect. "Whoever wants to be a leader among you must be your servant, and whoever wants to be first among you must become your slave. For even the Son of Man came not to be served but to serve others and to give His life as a ransom for many."[13]

On numerous occasions Jesus connected our calling to His: "Students are not greater than their teacher. But the student who is fully trained will become like the teacher."[14]

Face it. If Jesus were alive today He'd be on the Internet.

Wait a second! He is alive today!

He is on the Internet, living vicariously through His dedicated followers: loving, healing, caring and sharing His words of eternal life.[15]

The Apostle Peter frankly acknowledged that the options for humanity are seriously limited, "Lord, to whom would we go? You have the words that give eternal life."[16]

Now, those life-giving words have been given to us.

What will we do with them?

---

[12] Mark 16:15

[13] Matthew 20:26-28

[14] Luke 6:40

[15] John 3:16, 3:36, 4:14, 5:24, 6:27, 6:40, 6:47, Acts 13:46, Romans 6:22

[16] John 6:68

Will we preserve the words of life in a dead room protected by plastic Christianity? Or will we instead take the cover off so that men may come to know the living God who offers them infinite life?[17]

The Church must reach out to virtually everyone.

To do that, the Church must be Virtual.

CYBER CONVERSIONS

One of the most jolting conversations I ever had occurred in the fall of 2007, when I met a tech-savvy cyber evangelist from Campus Crusade ministry. He and his team had developed an Internet outreach that invited people to receive Jesus. Literally thousands from around the world responded everyday.

As I chatted with him, he scrolled through his iPhone showing me hundreds of people who, at that moment, wanted to know more about Jesus and how to be saved. He confessed that though it was exciting to witness such a continuously positive response, his heart grieved over the logistics. His ministry alone could not personally speak with each inquirer.

His request was simple: "I need hundreds of Christians who would spend five minutes a day online communicating with this fertile field of people. These hungry hearts just need words of encouragement from those who already know Jesus."

Hungry hearts just need words of encouragement from those who already know Jesus.

I left the conversation completely taken aback and convicted. Did I have the faith to believe that the people in our church family would be willing to spend five minutes a day, everyday, reaching those with outstretched hands from around the world?

---

17 Matthew 5:16

I wish I could say, "Yes". But I am asking for a further increase of faith and understanding of my role before I step into a place of meeting such a desperate need.

The words of Jesus have never been more accurate in assessing both the urgent cry and the staggering opportunity. Christ instructed His disciples: "The harvest is great, but the workers are few. So pray to the Lord who is in charge of the harvest; ask Him to send more workers into His fields."[18]

IS VIRTUAL REAL?

Virtual can be defined as "that which appears to exist, but is in fact—not real." It simulates or imitates actual life.

So the question can be rightfully asked, is it even possible for a healthy virtual church to exist?

The fact is, a virtual church has existed for quite some time.

In 2004, 64 percent of wired Americans (those using the Internet) had used the Internet for spiritual or religious purposes.[19]

Therefore, I believe it is more realistic and helpful to embrace the fact that, in some form, a virtual church already does exist, rather than deny and cease to cultivate it.

It reminds me of the inane term *illegitimate child*. Though I understand this phrase to be an ineffective attempt to discourage people from having babies outside of the marriage covenant, it ultimately places an absurd stigma on a child who has done nothing to merit such condescension. God the Father has no illegitimate children, only future adoptees into the wonderful family of God.[20]

---

18 Luke 10:2

19 Pew Internet & American Life Project, Stewart Hoover, Lynn Schofield Clark, Lee Rainie, 4/7/2004

20 Romans 8:15, Galatians 4:5, Ephesians 1:5

The virtual church has been birthed. It is not illegitimate. Though the virtual church will never replace the local church, it may be the only church for some. We must do all we can to embrace and integrate it into the Body of Christ. The cyber church will play an integral role, because "…this gospel of the kingdom will be preached in all the world as a witness to all the nations, and then the end will come."[21]

My final conversion to the reality of the virtual church happened in mid-2008. For less than a year we had been placing hundreds of short video excerpts online[22] on what has been called the next generation of television, Adobe Media Player. In one day we received over 450,000 hits from 174 nations. That was the day my debate over the Virtual Church ended. I accepted its permanent validity.

God the Father has no illegitimate children, only future adoptees into the wonderful family of God.

The only realistic and worthwhile question left was, "What can I do to help make the virtual church an authentic representation of Jesus Christ?"

The answer: spend the rest of my life doing all I can to, "…become all things to all men, that I might by all means save some."[23]

---

21 Matthew 24:14, NKJV

22 www.rockspots.tv

23 1Corinthians 9:22b

HOW FUTURISTS VIEW THE INTERNET

"A global, low-cost network will be thriving in 2020 and will be available to most people around the world..."[24]

This was the conviction of 48 percent of those who responded to a Pew Research Poll where, "Hundreds of Internet leaders, activists, builders and commentators were asked about the effect of the internet on social, political and economic life in the year 2020."

The majority agreed that "by 2020, this free flow of information will completely blur current national boundaries as they are replaced by city-states, corporation-based cultural groupings and/or other geographically diverse and reconfigured human organizations tied together by global networks."[25]

For better or worse, many Internet leaders believe "individuals' public and private lives will become increasingly 'transparent' globally. Everything will be more visible to everyone, with good and bad results."[26] We will discuss the benefits of intentional Spirit-directed transparency later in this chapter.

A near majority of Internet leaders believed that by 2020 the world will have leveled into "one big political, social and economic space in which people everywhere can meet and have verbal and visual exchanges regularly, face-to-face, over the internet."[27] It seems that the words, "face to face", refer to live images interacting on computer screens. Participants become instantly global, communicating in places never seen and with people never met.

---

24 Pew Research Polls Internet, The Future of the Internet II, September 24, 2006, Janna Quitney Anderson, Elon University

25 Ibid.

26 Ibid.

27 Ibid.

MIXED FRUIT

As I have grown older, and have seen much that startles me, I continue to be astounded at how two people can arrive at such diametrically opposite viewpoints. One person, based on his experience and belief, becomes an adamant atheist, while another chooses to be a whole-hearted follower of Jesus; one person sees skepticism as the best way to process life, while another sees faith in God as the way to higher ground.

Each is convinced the other is wrong.

Each holds tight to his convictions.

This contrast bears diverse fruit.

Two people can spend a comparable amount of time on the Internet. One is astounded by the wealth of insight at his fingertips. He can hardly pull himself away from the flood of revelation he gathers. Another spends the same amount of time surfing the net, but primarily in pornographic and salacious websites that rob him of his morals and dignity.

Browsing the Internet can be like snorkeling in a septic tank.

We can see that the Internet becomes different things to different people. That has more to do with each person's character than the Internet's content. For my own safety and protection, I installed software on my computer keeping me accountable to other men.

Programs like *xxxchurch.com* and *covenanteyes.com* can provide the safety net necessary in an age where browsing the Internet can be like snorkeling in a septic tank. I have too many people I love, who are looking to me as a man of integrity, to allow a former addiction to once again rule my heart.

With this safety net in place, I am able to spend many hours nearly everyday on the Internet, sometimes with worship music, but more often with the International House of Prayer's continuous worship and intercession playing in the background.[28]

At different times, while online, I read and write emails, conduct Bible studies, read the news headlines, view appropriate videos, dissect an area of interest, research a topic for a message or book, or worship and intercede in the Spirit. My experience with a safe connection to the Internet is a treasure chest of value assisting me in countless meaningful dimensions of my life. It is truly a blessing, not a curse.

NETWORKING NIRVANA OR NIGHTMARE

But all is not well in cyberspace.

At times, the boundary between the real and virtual worlds is very thin indeed.

Here are some cyber quotes from Internet experts who see the eminent dangers of this brave new world of virtual reality.

- "Privacy is a thing of the past."[29]
- "There is a strong likelihood that virtual reality will become less virtual and more reality for many."[30]
- "Multiple personalities will become commonplace, and cyber-psychiatry will proliferate."[31]
- "A human's desire is to reinvent himself, live out his fantasies, overindulge; addiction will definitely increase. Whole communities/subcultures, which even today

---

28 You can sign up and enjoy IHOP's constant stream of worship and prayer on your own computer by visiting www.ihop.org

29 Hal Varian, University of California-Berkeley and Google

30 Barry Chudakov, principal, The Chudakov Company

31 Daniel Wang, principal partner, Roadmap Associates

are a growing faction, will materialize. We may see a vast blurring of virtual/real reality with many participants living an in-effect secluded lifestyle. Only in the online world will they participate in any form of human interaction."[32]

- "Before 2020, every newborn child in industrialized countries will be implanted with an RFID or similar chip. Ostensibly providing important personal and medical data, these may also be used for tracking and surveillance."[33] This was the observation of one professor from Israel in light of the Bible's future prediction of an Anti-Christ,[34] and the Mark of the Beast.[35]

- "It will NOT be a better world. It will be an Orwellian world! The benefits most certainly will not outweigh the costs."[36]

There were times in each of our lives when the lines between reality and fantasy blurred. From emotional infatuations to innocent daydreams, we have each wistfully lamented what was never intended for us. Our reveries often crush the real and genuine and leave us disillusioned with the God of truth.

"Thousands of years ago, Roman naturalist Pliny expressed one of the earliest interests in perceptual illusion when he wrote about an artist who had 'produced a picture of grapes so dexterously represented that birds began to fly down to eat from the painted vine.'"[37]

---

32 Robert Eller, technology consultant

33 Michael Dahan, a professor at Sapir Academic College in Israel

34 Revelation 13

35 Revelation 16:2, 19:20

36 Sharon Lane, president of WebPageDesign

37 Biocca F, Kim T Levy M. The Vision of Virtual Reality. In Biocca, Levy, ed. *Communication in the Age of Virtual Reality* (Lawrence Erlbaum Associates, 1995:3–14).

We are each prone to deception. As the songwriter once wrote, "Prone to wander, Lord, I feel it. Prone to leave the God I love; here's my heart, O take and seal it. Seal it for Thy courts above."[38]

Scores of industry insiders voice cyber cautions and concerns. They see first-hand patterns of destructive tendencies and behaviors among their peers. As the level of technical expertise moves us closer and closer to a nearly indistinguishable separation between the real and imagined, many will be pulled into emotional enslavement.

Once again, those within the industry well know the slippery slope of virtual technology. Here are some of their concerns:

- "I already see many internet junkies who need a fix…"[39]
- "As the quality of virtual reality increases, it will attract more users and the number of cyber-addicts will increase."[40]
- "Simulations will develop to where some players' experiences so closely mimic reality that the players will be stimulated with the same neurotransmitters that drive feelings of love and pleasure in the real world. There will be simulations as addictive as nicotine and cocaine…"[41]
- "Addiction to chat rooms and online gaming worlds is already emerging as an issue. Recent research has highlighted for example, how teenagers' ability to learn during school hours is being impacted by a lack of sleep—caused by late-night SMS/chat sessions. There is a real risk that some people will become 'lost' to virtual worlds."[42]

---

[38] Come, Thou Fount of Every Blessing, words by Robert Robinson, 1758, music by John Wyeth, 1813

[39] Tiffany Shlain, founder of the Webby Awards

[40] Thomas Lenzo, Internet consultant

[41] Sean Mead, a technology consultant

[42] Heath Gibson, competitive intelligence analyst for BigPond in Australia

- "Reality will be one seamless world that spans face-to-face and digital areas of action."[43]
- "The distinction between 'real' and 'virtual' realities will continue to blur... Our definitions of what is 'real' will be tested and changed."[44]

Some, believing massive online addictions are inevitable, recommend the equivalent of cyber methadone recovery programs, forming online communities to assist people with Internet addictions.

One addiction expert wrote, "I have studied addiction for 36 years. We already have millions who are addicts. The issue is not to regulate them but to offer a life in which such behavior is not needed, and that, too, can be accomplished on the Internet. We need to create valuable and helpful communities on the Web that will allow millions to connect."[45]

So what do we do as virtual missionaries on the forefront of a potentially destructive frontier?

The same thing we should do in any broken culture that needs Jesus.

We love, we minister, we serve, and bring God's Kingdom to Earth.

---

[43] Ted Coopman of the University of Washington

[44] Martin Kwapinski, senior content manager for FirstGov, the U.S. Government's official Web portal

[45] Addiction expert Walter J. Broadbent of The Broadbent Group

CYBER CURE: COMMUNITY

In September 2008, social networking sites such as MySpace and Facebook surpassed porn sites for number of hits. According to Bill Tancer, a self-described "data geek," porn searches have dropped to about 10 percent of searches from 20 percent a decade ago.[46] Noting that, in particular, the 18–24 year old age group was searching less for porn, Tancer said, "My theory is that young users spend so much time on social networks that they don't have time to look at adult sites."

> **God intentionally makes Himself hidden, but highly accessible.**

What a perfect opportunity for the Church to find her relational place in the cyber community! While links to specific social networks will vary within both secular and church-related communities, a vital connection will provide extraordinary opportunities to share the love and life of Jesus with people locally and globally.

God intentionally makes Himself hidden, but highly accessible. Eager to be revealed and longing for relationship, He sets the stage for a covenant with us on His terms, for His glory, and for our good.

This relational intimacy with our invisible Creator is being tapped by millions of Christians on a daily basis. "You love Him even though you have never seen Him. Though you do not see Him now, you trust Him; and you rejoice with a glorious, inexpressible joy."[47]

Is it not possible to have a valuable connection through emails, blogs and videos with people across the world? A divine dialogue is about to swell to new depths. The secular culture has already tapped into its value. Now, it's time for the church to discern her role.

---

46 Tancer B. *Click: What Millions of People are Doing Online and Why It Matters* (Hyperion, 2008).
47 1Peter 1:8

VIRTUAL POSSES ARE WATCHING

The book, *Who Controls the Internet?*, states that "[China] is trying to create an Internet that is free enough to support and maintain the world's fastest growing economy yet closed enough to tamp down political threats to its monopoly on power."[48]

"China reportedly employs as many as 50,000 internet investigators who conduct online surveillance, erasing commentary, blocking sites, and authorizing the arrests of people for any communication that is seen to be unpatriotic."[49]

Big brother is not just watching in China, many Muslim nations report similar controls, with arrests and imprisonments becoming more frequent.

My reason for mentioning the increase in Internet censorship is to highlight the fact that the present open cyber-door of communication may eventually close. Inhabitants of nations that are right now able and eager to hear the undiluted truth of God's great news will eventually lose that ability.

Jesus Himself acknowledged the temporary nature of open doors: "We must quickly carry out the tasks assigned us by the One who sent us. The night is coming, and then no one can work."[50]

May we not miss this divine appointment.

---

48 Goldsmith J, Wu T. *Who Controls the Internet? Illusions of a Borderless World* (Oxford University Press, 2005:89).

49 French H. As Chinese Students Go Online, Little Sister is Watching. New York Times. May 9, 2006. Available at http://www.nytimes.com/2006/05/09/world/asia/09internet.html. Last accessed July 15, 2009.

50 John 9:4

VIRTUAL GATE KEEPERS

As time goes on, many of you reading will come to accept the reality that God is inviting, perhaps asking you to have a Holy Spirit directed connection with the Internet. Here are some options for you to prayerfully consider:

Internet Churches

Local churches will form additional trans-local campuses with interested participants from around the globe, allowing a cultural cross-pollination, with previously unthinkable possibilities. One church that has pioneered Internet Campuses is *lifechurch.tv* with main offices in Edmund, Oklahoma. A visit to their website will provide a glimpse into the future of Internet churches.

Online Messages

Teaching and preaching in both topical and expository presentations will provide ongoing instruction and impartation to anyone, anywhere in the world. These messages will be available in various formats: audio or video digital-media: presently CD's, DVD's, HD, podcasts, and streaming media. Only God knows about future technologies that will further expedite the communication of the gospel.

Small Groups

Likewise, on a trans-local level, there will be many creative opportunities to connect with other believers in a global relational community and share life together. Obviously, attendees must establish safe parameters to guard against relational, financial, or doctrinal hazards.

Blogging

A blog is a contraction of the term "Web log." It is a website, created and maintained by an individual. The blogger makes regular entries of content, graphics, photos and videos. As of 2008, there were an estimated 200 million blogs worldwide.

On a blog entitled, *Some Reasons Why I Nearly Quit Blogging*, one blogger listed some helpful suggestions for creating and maintaining a blog.

- Think long term rather than short term.
- Don't expect instant success.
- Don't quit your day job on day one.
- Expect to work hard on quality content and quality networking.
- Blogging in a vacuum sucks.

Personal Testimonies

Sharing the mighty work God has done in your life is another way of offering God's free gift. In our own local church meetings individuals share a five-minute My Story each week. Some of these are now viewable around the world on the Internet.

As was expounded upon in the *Transparent Church* chapter, I am convinced the World Wide Web will play a significant role in the future fulfillment of the Great Commission,[51] "And they overcame him by the blood of the Lamb and by the word of their testimony, and they did not love their lives to the death."[52]

---

51 Matthew 24:14

52 Revelation 12:11, NKJV

Video Testimonies

Since the advent of video sharing websites like YouTube in 2005, multiple millions of short videos are available for free viewing. All estimates are that this will continue to increase exponentially.

Cyber-Pastors and Coaches

The need for leadership within these cyber-communities is evident. God will raise-up mature spiritual guides who will provide the directional oversight for the unlimited opportunities and challenges ahead.

Fathers and Mothers

In the climactic days prior to His return, God is restoring the relational connection between parents and children in a marvelous way. It was predicted long ago, and must be fulfilled at the end of the age.

The Spirit of God spoke through the prophet Malachi, "Look, I am sending you the prophet Elijah before the great and dreadful day of the LORD arrives. His preaching will turn the hearts of fathers to their children, and the hearts of children to their fathers. Otherwise I will come and strike the land with a curse."[53]

God is calling spiritual dads and moms who are willing to reach around the globe with hearts of adoption, to embrace the fatherless and orphans. At times this can and will be done in person. But with the availability of the Internet to spiritual parents, globetrotting with God's Father heart will open up whole new mission fields.

---

[53] Malachi 4:5–6

Celebrity Prayers

Data geek, Bill Tancer also noted that the present obsession with celebrities and celebrity websites produces more hits than religion, politics, diet, and wellbeing sites combined. There appears to be no sign of celebrity mania waning. With this in mind, God desires to open doors to reach celebrities and their fans.[54]

Recently we had a series of messages entitled, *What Hollywood Believes*, in which we addressed various celebrity beliefs about God, Jesus, the Bible, etc. Certain individuals, burdened to pray for celebrities, posted a video of their celebrity prayers on *rockspots.tv*. Their comments and prayers were positive, personal, and even prophetic. This wide-open mission field deserves prayerful consideration.

To the Ends of the Earth

There has never been a greater opportunity for the fulfillment of the final words of Jesus prior to His ascension into Heaven, "But you will receive power when the Holy Spirit comes upon you. And you will be My witnesses, telling people about Me everywhere—in Jerusalem, throughout Judea, in Samaria, and to the ends of the earth."[55]

What a day!

What an opportunity!

It's great to be alive!

*Addendum to Chapter 7 found on page 251

---

54 Tancer B. *Click: What Millions of People are Doing Online and Why It Matters* (Hyperion, 2008).
55 Acts 1:8

QUESTIONS FOR DISCUSSION

1. Is technology assisting or hindering your walk with God?

2. Do you believe God is using the Internet to reach people for Him, and will this increase?

3. Have you personally used the Internet to grow spiritually?

4. How do you suppose God views Internet safe-guarding?

5. Can you imagine yourself being a part of a healthy social network or Christian community on the Internet?

6. Have you ever considered the Internet as a mission field? What would that look like for you?

8 PERSECUTED CHURCH

CHAPTER EIGHT

"Great faith is the product of great fights. Great testimonies are the outcome of great tests. Great triumphs can only come out of great trials."

SMITH WIGGLESWORTH

THE LONG NIGHT AHEAD

God will continue to shake all that can be shaken around and within us, "…so that only unshakable things will remain."[1] We are being brought to the realization that unless God intervenes on Earth, the planet will destroy itself and God's people as well. Jesus made this quite clear, "In fact, unless that time of calamity is shortened, not a single person will survive. But it will be shortened for the sake of God's chosen ones."[2]

In my early Christian life I thought many of the challenges faced by first century Christians were somehow not relevant in the twentieth century. However, the struggles of Paul and other apostles seem to be less remote and more likely with the passage of time. Here is Paul's account of the battle he faced:

> "We are pressed on every side by troubles, but we are not crushed. We are perplexed, but not driven to despair. We are hunted down, but never abandoned by God. We get knocked down, but we are not destroyed.

---

[1] Hebrews 12:27a

[2] Matthew 24:22

> *Through suffering, our bodies continue to share in the death of Jesus so that the life of Jesus may also be seen in our bodies. Yes, we live under constant danger of death because we serve Jesus, so that the life of Jesus will be evident in our dying bodies. So we live in the face of death, but this has resulted in eternal life for you. But we continue to preach because we have the same kind of faith the psalmist had when he said, 'I believed in God, so I spoke.'"*[3]

Today, many nations would affirm Paul's depiction as an accurate account of dramatic challenges Christians regularly face. What is unique to our day is the level of persecution against formerly Christianized nations in Western Europe.

Paul, in his letter to Timothy, further elaborates the condition of the End Time culture:

> "You should know this, Timothy, that in the last days there will be very difficult times. For people will love only themselves and their money. They will be boastful and proud, scoffing at God, disobedient to their parents, and ungrateful. They will consider nothing sacred. They will be unloving and unforgiving; they will slander others and have no self-control. They will be cruel and hate what is good. They will betray their friends, be reckless, be puffed up with pride, and love pleasure rather than God. They will act religious, but they will reject the power that could make them godly. Stay away from people like that!"[4]

One of the great ironies in life is that, even if we act above reproach, others may not notice. In any case, we cannot forget, "We serve God whether people honor us or despise us, whether they slander us or praise us. We are honest, but they call us impostors."[5] In the end, we live for an audience of One.

---

[3] 2Corinthians 4:8–13

[4] 2Timothy 3:1–5

[5] 2Corinthians 6:8

HEALTHY HABITS OR RELIGIOUS RUTS

America is one of the unhealthiest societies on the planet.

We eat too much, exercise too little, accumulate stress and are depleted of sleep. We're eating, sitting, and stressing ourselves to death. An annual survey, conducted by the American Psychological Association, found that 80 percent of Americans worry about their personal finances and the economy.[6]

Are our spiritual habits any better?

I think not.

Most people fear the future, wallow in the past, and lack peace for the present. Many Christians are spiritually unhealthy, void of the true rest that comes from trusting God. In essence, we fail to discern God's heart for us and lose sight of our true identity.

Do we, as followers of the Prince of Peace,[7] abide in the peace that goes beyond our understanding?[8] Are our lives filled with the inexpressible joy that was experienced by Christians of other ages?[9] Is the rest that comes from knowing God part of our daily lives?[10] If these healthy dimensions are absent, then what do we have that resembles the abundant and superior life Jesus promised?[11]

Unhealthy spiritual habits and religious ruts pose the most dangerous approach to meeting daunting challenges ahead. Jesus calls us to blast out of the faithless fog that paralyzes our perspective, into the extraordinary life He promised us and He Himself lived while on this Earth.

---

6 April through September 2008 Survey, American Psychological Association, 7,000 respondents
7 Isaiah 9:6
8 Philippians 4:7
9 1Peter 1:8
10 Psalm 37:7
11 John 10:10

Jesus calls us to blast out of the faithless fog that paralyzes our perspective, into the extraordinary life He promised us and He Himself lived while on this Earth.

Anytime I've had problems with my computer and asked for help from one of our techies, the first thing he'll ask me is, "Have you restarted your computer?" Most of the time this simple procedure resolves the issue. For some reason, I often forget this solution.

So too in the Spirit realm. If you're stuck, reboot. Repent and change direction. Renew your commitment. Resolve to allow God to restore the missing link to abundant life.

The religious leaders in Christ's day were so stuck perpetuating pointless rituals, that He couldn't help but reprove them, "What sorrow awaits you teachers of religious law and you Pharisees. Hypocrites! For you are so careful to clean the outside of the cup and the dish, but inside you are filthy—full of greed and self-indulgence!"[12] If there is little or no life in you, reboot.

Most of the time, in order to get up and out, we have to go down and in—humbling ourselves and asking the Lord to show us what needs to change. It is always a stretching process but eventually yields "...the light that leads to life."[13]

Perhaps the most essential ingredient to remaining truly healthy in these unsettling times is flexibility: the ability to stretch without breaking, to change without resisting, to flow without missing a divine opportunity. Healthy tree limbs bend. Dead branches break. The church will face stretching ahead, requiring conscious willingness to be retooled by the hand of God, that only fully yielded hearts will finish well.

Paul the Apostle knew the significance of yielding to God and finishing well. He wrote, "But my life is worth nothing to me unless I use it for finishing the work assigned me by the

---

12 Matthew 23:25

13 John 8:12b

Lord Jesus—the work of telling others the Good News about the wonderful grace of God."[14]

King Solomon, in one of his most surrendered moments, prayed, "Therefore give to Your servant an understanding heart to judge Your people, that I may discern between good and evil."[15] He knew he needed discernment, flexibility, and willingness to yield to the slightest promptings of God's Spirit. How tragic that this same brilliant leader would fall into complete deception. "For it was so, when Solomon was old, that his wives turned his heart after other gods; and his heart was not loyal to the LORD his God, as was the heart of his father David."[16] Though he had tasted and seen the Lord's goodness,[17] he lost his hunger and thirst for God's best.[18]

Stay flexible! Be willing to adapt to the flow of God's Spirit in any given moment. "Therefore submit (yield) to God. Resist the devil and he will flee from you."[19] We are all headed for the new and unfamiliar: the grand finale of the Battle for Earth. We will not be defeated unless we foolishly venture alone, or refuse to follow God's leading. For "…the Spirit of truth, has come, He will guide you into all truth; for He will not speak on His own authority, but whatever He hears He will speak; and He will tell you things to come."[20]

The most challenging tests incite God's best for us.

The righteous flee forward!

Which direction are you headed?

The most essential ingredient to remaining truly healthy in these unsettling times is flexibility.

---

14 Acts 20:24

15 1Kings 3:9a, NKJV

16 1Kings 11:4

17 Psalm 34:8

18 Matthew 5:6

19 James 4:7, NKJV (emphasis mine.)

20 John 16:13, NKJV

THE LAST FLIGHT OUT

An unknown author from the second century wrote the following to describe Christians to the Romans:

> "They dwell in their own countries simply as sojourners... They are in the flesh, but they do not live after the flesh. They pass their days on earth, but they are citizens of heaven. They obey the prescribed laws, and at the same time, they surpass the laws by their lives. They love all men but are persecuted by all. They are unknown and condemned. They are put to death, but [will be] restored to life. They are poor, yet they make many rich. They possess few things; yet, they abound in all. They are dishonored, but in their very dishonor are glorified... And those who hate them are unable to give any reason for their hatred." [21]

Justin Martyr, one of the early church leaders, explained to the Romans, "Since our thoughts are not fixed on the present, we are not concerned when men put us to death. Death is a debt we must all pay anyway."[22] He compared the love of Christians before and after their conversions. "We who used to value the acquisition of wealth and possessions more than anything else now bring what we have into a common fund and share it with anyone who needs it. We used to hate and destroy one another and refused to associate with people of another race or country. Now, because of Christ, we live together with such people and pray for our enemies."[23]

Author David Bercot provides an overview of life in the Early Church. "The supreme example of their absolute trust in God was their acceptance of persecution. From the time of the Emperor Trajan (around A.D. 100) until the Edict of Milan was

---

[21] Unknown author Letter to Diognetus Chap.5
[22] Justin First Apology chap. 11
[23] Justin First Apology chap. 14

issued in 313, the practice of Christianity was illegal within the boundaries of the Roman Empire. Being a Christian was a crime punishable by death. But the Roman officials didn't generally hunt out Christians. They ignored them unless someone formally accused a person of being a Christian. As a result, persecution was intermittent. Christians in one town would suffer horrible tortures and death while Christians in a nearby area would be untouched. It was totally unpredictable. Yet, every Christian lived daily with a death sentence hanging over his head."[24]

Even the adversaries of early Christians were stunned by how they lived. One pagan commented: "They despise the temples as houses of the dead. They reject the gods. They laugh at sacred things. Wretched, they pity our priests. Half naked themselves, they despise honors and purple robes. What incredible audacity and foolishness! They are not afraid of present torments, but they fear those that are uncertain and future. While they do not fear to die for the present, they fear to die after death…"[25]

Would we as modern day Christians be accused of such radical faith?

Some might think, "I hope not!"

Scripture, in contrast, paints a clear picture of how history's greatest lived and died:

> *"By faith these people overthrew kingdoms, ruled with justice, and received what God had promised them. They shut the mouths of lions, quenched the flames of fire, and escaped death by the edge of the sword. Their weakness was turned to strength. They became strong*

---

[24] Bercot DW. *Will the Real Heretics Please Stand Up: A New Look at Today's Evangelical Church in the Light of Early Christianity* (Scroll Publishing Company, 1989).

[25] M. Felix Octavius chaps. 8, 12

> *in battle and put whole armies to flight. Women received their loved ones back again from death. But others were tortured, refusing to turn from God in order to be set free. They placed their hope in a better life after the resurrection. Some were jeered at, and their backs were cut open with whips. Others were chained in prisons. Some died by stoning, some were sawed in half, and others were killed with the sword. Some went about wearing skins of sheep and goats, destitute and oppressed and mistreated. They were too good for this world, wandering over deserts and mountains, hiding in caves and holes in the ground."*[26]

What once impressed God as a pure demonstration of faith and love is still what He's looking for. David W. Bercot describes the stark difference between third century Christianity and its society in his book, *Will The Real Heretics Please Stand Up*. "When a devastating plague swept across the ancient world in the third century, Christians were the only ones who cared for the sick, which they did at the risk of contracting the plague themselves. Meanwhile, pagans were throwing infected members of their own families into the streets even before they died, in order to protect themselves from the disease."[27]

I believe, in the years to come, the most compelling attraction drawing non-Christians to Jesus will be the selfless response to persecution by genuine Christ followers. The love of God always invites attention. Bercot comments, "…most new believers didn't have to be warned about the coming suffering. They had seen it for themselves. In fact, one of the most powerful means of evangelism in the early church was the example of the thousands of Christians who endured suffering and death because they refused to deny Christ."[28]

---

26 Hebrews 11:33–38

27 Eusebius History of the Church bk. 7, chap. 22

28 Bercot DW. *Will the Real Heretics Please Stand Up: A New Look at Today's Evangelical Church in the Light of Early Christianity* (Scroll Publishing Company, 1989).

Dr. Martin Luther King echoed this same strategy: "We will match your capacity to inflict suffering with our capacity to endure suffering. We will meet your physical force with soul force. We will not hate you, but we will not obey your evil laws. We will soon wear you down by pure capacity to suffer."

God, give us this kind of faith-filled endurance.

> "We will match your capacity to inflict suffering with our capacity to endure suffering."
>
> —Dr Martin Luther King

STATE-SPONSORED CHRISTIAN CHURCHES

Never forget two essential realities that will provide much understanding during the treacherous days ahead:

1. Our Founder was murdered. The most loving Person who ever lived, was hated and killed because He was envied.[29]
2. The demonic forces that killed Jesus are still around. They will martyr members of the End Time church out of jealousy,[30] and not because we are hypocritical, insincere, prejudiced, boring, or faultfinding.

Here's how I believe the next phase will play out.

Within 20 years, significant portions of the Holy Bible, and much of the Christian church in the Western World, once considered mainstream, will be first persecuted and then outlawed.

A politically correct version of the Old and New Testament will alter and even eliminate many controversial verses (e.g. scriptures that pertain to sexual morality, sexual identity, marriage between a man and a woman, Jesus being the only way,

---

[29] Matthew 27:18, Mark 15:10

[30] Acts 13:45, 17:5, Romans 1:29, Titus 3:3

and other dimensions of moral purity). Significant portions of the original Bible, transcribed and translated for thousands of years, will be considered "hate literature." Legislation will ban the printing and propagation of many of the genuine versions of the Scripture.

Under the guise of a worldwide effort to promote a new level of harmony and mutual respect, revisions will weed out so-called prejudices. This distortion itself will wear the mask of God's love. A new concept of "God" will introduce the entire civilized world to a He/She who loves and accepts all people and their chosen life styles. Previous views of God—a God of judgment—will be deemed misrepresentations of His/Her true nature. Much of the planet will applaud this God and Bible facelift.

Churches who continue to use the prohibited versions of Scripture will lose their tax-exempt status, be ostracized from their communities, and will even be subject to litigation and prosecution. Lawsuits, both civil and criminal, will be filed against denominations, churches, and leaders of churches. Christian leaders will be prosecuted, fined and sent to jail. Over time, much of the genuine church in the Western World will be forced to worship and teach underground.

Out of our deepest struggles will emerge our finest hour!

This politically correct "Christian" church, and its heretical version of the Bible, will become the universal form of Christianity, recognized as the original that Jesus Himself espoused. Bible-based Christianity will be considered an aberration needing correction, much like the Crusades or Salem Witch Trials. Society will judge this realignment of the "fundamentalist" brand of Christianity a major breakthrough in understanding. "At last," they will say, "the errant misrepresentation of Jesus Christ is correct." The modern mindset will embrace this new and improved Jesus as the perfect role model.

With the approval of the apostate church, the stage is prepared for the entrance of the one-world government and the Anti-Christ.

The Bible foretold this: "Now the Spirit expressly says that in latter times some will depart from the faith, giving heed to deceiving spirits and doctrines of demons, speaking lies in hypocrisy, having their own conscience seared with a hot iron…"[31]

Jesus likewise clearly predicted nearly 2,000 years ago, "Then you will be arrested, persecuted, and killed. You will be hated all over the world because you are My followers. And many will turn away from Me and betray and hate each other. And many false prophets will appear and will deceive many people. Sin will be rampant everywhere, and the love of many will grow cold. But the one who endures to the end will be saved. And the Good News about the Kingdom will be preached throughout the whole world, so that all nations will hear it; and then the end will come."[32]

We must not consider these startling events a challenge to reluctantly wait for but an opportunity to earnestly prepare for. A clear division of Bible-believing Christians from false will signal the birth of the legitimate End Time Church.

In preparation for these events, we must redeem the time, brace our spirits and train our souls to respond as Jesus did. As we lay down our lives for a hate-filled, embittered culture, we will see a great harvest of those who will discern the gravity of the eleventh hour. We will witness the grandest of all opportunities to represent the God of love as we flow in the often unseen fruit of God's Spirit: longsuffering, kindness, goodness, faithfulness, gentleness and self-control.[33]

---

[31] 1Timothy 4:1–2
[32] Matthew 24:9–14
[33] Galatians 5:22–23

> **The enemy will deceive multitudes into believing their archenemy is Bible-believing Christians.**

As the Bible then says, "There is no law against these things! Those who belong to Christ Jesus have nailed the passions and desires of their sinful nature to His cross and crucified them there. Since we are living by the Spirit, let us follow the Spirit's leading in every part of our lives."[34]

Out of our deepest struggles will emerge our finest hour!

THE SEQUENCE OF PERSECUTION

Make no mistake. There has always been a need and a call for blood in the spirit realm. Why? Because the Bible says that life is in the blood.[35]

In the years to come, the willingness of Christ's disciples to shed their own blood will demonstrate true motives. "For consider Him who endured such hostility from sinners against Himself, lest you become weary and discouraged in your souls. You have not yet resisted to bloodshed, striving against sin."[36] It is the blood of God the Son that calls men to return to their Creator. Christ's premeditated death set the pattern of complete surrender for all sincere hearts that would come after Him.

In stark contrast, the devil's unquenchable thirst for blood—in particular, the blood of martyrs for Jesus—will punctuate the climax of the age. The enemy will deceive multitudes into believing their archenemy is Bible-believing Christians. Though nothing could be further from the truth, much of humanity will believe this lie for "…Satan disguises himself as an angel of

---

34 Galatians 5:23b–25, NKJV

35 Leviticus 17:14

36 Hebrews 12:3–4, NKJV

light."[37] It will seek to rid the planet of perceived antagonists against the unity, peace and love it seeks.

The sacrificial deaths of genuine Christian martyrs will solicit applause from both Hell and Heaven—but for polar reasons.

Hell will applaud their deaths thinking this is the end of the matter. Heaven, on the other hand, will see the purity of their motives and the fulfillment of God's eternal purpose. It will applaud in affirmation that God's chosen ones have paid the ultimate price of surrender to the Father's will. In the end, these purposeful deaths will liberate multitudes who see God's heart demonstrated by sacrificial love.

Jesus affirmed this sequence of surrender, "If you refuse to take up your cross and follow Me, you are not worthy of being Mine. If you cling to your life, you will lose it; but if you give up your life for Me, you will find it."[38]

SEPARATION OF CHURCH AND FATE

As of June 2008, a Pew Forum on Religion and Public Life survey found that only 5 percent of Americans said they did not believe in God, while 3 percent didn't know. A full 71 percent were absolutely certain that God existed, and 17 percent were fairly certain.[39]

At first glance this survey might seem quite encouraging, but a closer examination reveals a troubling trend. While many Americans still believe in God, individual concepts of God Himself have significantly diverged from a purely biblical perspective. In addition, belief in the Bible as the inerrant and inspired Word of God continues to decrease.

---

37 2Corinthians 11:4

38 Matthew 10:38–39

39 June 23, 2008 survey by the Pew Forum on Religion & Public Life based on interviews with more than 35,000 Americans ages 18 and older.

Out of the 35,556 people surveyed by this Pew Forum on Religion and Public Life:

- 33% believe the Bible is the Word of God, and is literally true word for word.
- 30% believe the Bible is the Word of God, but not literally true word for word.
- 28% believe the Bible is a Book written by men, and not the word of God.
- 9% don't know what to believe, or refused to answer the question.

In 1984, a Gallup survey determined that 38 percent of Americans believed the Bible is the actual word of God. As was documented in the first chapter entitled, *Dying Church*, an even smaller percentage of those who say they believe the Bible is literally true, have a biblical worldview. From this downward shift we can see that our principle danger is not a disbelief in God, but rather a gradual ignorance and subsequent rejection of the Holy Bible. This reinterpretation or, in reality, this misinterpretation creates a fictitious God made in the image of man. Once the Bible is removed as the accurate standard by which truth is gauged, all pillars of belief and practice begin to crumble.

God's Word is the exclusive accurate spiritual compass. Those who abandon or marginalize it will eventually dismiss it, and consequently move further away from the God of reality. The psalmist knew all to well, "Your word is a lamp to guide my feet and a light for my path."[40]

If we compromise our Scriptural foundation, we will find ourselves reinventing truth and fostering deception. "All Scripture is inspired by God and is useful to teach us what is true and to

---

[40] Psalm 119:105

make us realize what is wrong in our lives. It corrects us when we are wrong and teaches us to do what is right."[41]

Efforts to define truth that conflict with the Bible always lead to gross error. Likewise, attempts to live outside of God's best for our lives will produce emptiness and futility.

Jesus, the eternal Word made flesh[42] guaranteed that, "Heaven and earth will disappear, but My words will never disappear."[43] The choice of fully receiving and embracing the Bible is before us.

LOVING LIKE JESUS

Jesus made an extraordinary statement that definitively separates authentic Christianity from all other religions. He said, "But to you who are willing to listen, I say, love your enemies! Do good to those who hate you. Bless those who curse you. Pray for those who hurt you. If someone slaps you on one cheek, offer the other cheek also."[44]

Then Jesus added a sentence so profound, it has been called the golden rule: "Do to others as you would like them to do to you. If you love only those who love you, why should you get credit for that? Even sinners love those who love them! And if you do good only to those who do good to you, why should you get credit? Even sinners do that much!"[45]

The heart of God the Father says: "Love your enemies! Do good to them. Lend to them without expecting to be repaid. Then your reward from heaven will be very great, and you will truly be acting as children of the Most High, for He is kind to

---

41 2Timothy 3:16

42 John 1:1,14

43 Mark 13:31

44 Luke 6:27–29a

45 Luke 6:31–33

The only cure for hatred is love.

those who are unthankful and wicked. You must be compassionate, just as your Father is compassionate."[46]

The only cure for hatred is love.

Though the Old Testament did teach, "…love your neighbor as yourself,"[47] over time, religious leaders added "and hate your enemies." To rectify this distortion of God's heart, Jesus qualified our neighbor as everyone! So we are to love everyone, even our enemies, returning the love God has so freely given to us. Only then are we most like Him who unconditionally loves all people. True love alone mirrors the God of love. The Bible affirms this marvelous equation: "Love does no wrong to others, so love fulfills the requirements of God's law."[48]

It is not a coincidence that Dr. King lived and wrote about this message of loving your enemies:

> "I believe that unarmed truth and unconditional love will have the final word in reality. That is why right, temporarily defeated, is stronger than evil triumphant. Hatred paralyzes life; love releases it. Hatred confuses life; love harmonizes it. Hatred darkens life; love illuminates it. Let no man pull you low enough to hate him.
>
> "I have decided to love. If you are seeking the highest good, I think you can find it through love. And the beautiful thing is that we are moving against wrong when we do it, because John was right, God is love. He who hates does not know God, but he who has love has the key that unlocks the door to the meaning of ultimate reality."

---

[46] Luke 6:35–36

[47] Leviticus 19:18b

[48] Romans 13:10

EMBRACING OFFENSE

One step ahead and you are a hero; two steps ahead and you're a martyr.

We are coming into a two-step age.

As evidence of the twisted thinking that will shape the coming season, some liberal journalists consider smoking and obesity greater moral issues than abortion. They cite that unborn babies have no "claim to be born."[49]

In December 2008, an atheist group called the Freedom From Religion Foundation was given permission to place an anti-religion sign next to a Nativity scene—part of Washington state's official holiday display. The sign read: "There are no gods, no devils, no angels, no heaven or hell. There is only our natural world. Religion is but myth and superstition that hardens hearts and enslaves minds."

In the years to come, harsh value judgments will be made concerning the supposed dangers Bible-believing Christians pose to society. Anticipate a culture anxious to ostracize for "unreasonable," "irrational" and "unacceptable" beliefs.

Dr. Albert Mohler describes new attempts to marginalize the Christian message in his book, *Culture Shift*, "A new and unprecedented right is now the central focus of legal, procedural, and cultural concern in many corridors—a supposed right not to be offended. The risk of being offended is simply part of what it means to live in a diverse culture that honors and celebrates free speech. Those who now claim to be offended are generally speaking of an emotional state that has resulted from some real or perceived insult to their belief system or from contact with someone else's belief system. Now, 'the right never to be offended' is not only accepted as legitimate, but is actually promoted by the media, by government, and by activist groups."[50]

---

49 Pollitt K. Prochoice Puritans. The Nation. February 13, 2006.
　Available at http://www.thenation.com/doc/20060213/pollitt. Last accessed July 15, 2009.

50 *Culture Shift: Engaging Current Issues with Timeless Truth*, R. Albert Mohler Jr.

We have already discussed how, at times, Christians offend those outside the faith by inappropriate behavior. This type of offense is completely unacceptable and indefensible. But this is not the context of offense Dr. Mohler describes. He continues, "...there is no way for a faithful Christian to avoid offending those who are offended by Jesus Christ and His cross. The truth claims of Christianity, by their very particularity and exclusivity, are inherently offensive to those who would demand some other gospel."[51]

"When Paul spoke of the Cross as 'foolishness' and a 'stumbling block',[52] he was pointing to this reality—a reality that would lead to his own stoning, flogging, imprisonment, and execution."[53] The very nature of the gospel offends the unregenerate mind.

The very nature of the gospel offends the unregenerate mind.

There is inconsistency between the desires of our flesh and the holiness of God. Offense can actually be seen as a point of contention between the Spirit of God and sinful man.

How do we react to having our mind offended by a God who is bigger than our understanding? What's our response when our flesh is offended by a God who is perfectly holy? Do we numb our consciences with the painkiller of "a right to not be offended"? Do we placate our addiction to comfort by saying, "God is a gentleman and would never make me feel uncomfortable"? Or do we embrace conviction and die to ourselves?

Choosing to die is not easy. But everything is easier after you're dead! You cannot offend a dead man. Jesus said, "God blesses those who are not offended by Me."[54]

---

51 *Culture Shift: Engaging Current Issues with Timeless Truth*, R. Albert Mohler Jr.
52 1Corinthians 1:23, NIV
53 *Culture Shift: Engaging Current Issues with Timeless Truth*, R. Albert Mohler Jr.
54 Matthew 11:6

May we be wise and humble enough to let the Cross be the offense and not our own insensitivities.

FALSE COMFORT

In the coming season, while being "hard-pressed on every side…perplexed… persecuted [and] struck down,"[55] we must continually be on guard against bad theology and false comfort. The first of these defective options will leave us deceived, while the second will instill artificial assurance.

I experienced a false sense of comfort during the height of the Cuban Missile Crisis, in the fall of 1962. I was just 13 years old. The threat of a thermo-nuclear holocaust with the Soviet Union seemed imminent. In preparation for possible radioactive fall-out, our 7th grade class practiced crawling under desks. Such a strategy might have protected some of us from falling debris, but is ineffective against lethal weapons of mass destruction. Too little too late.

In a comparable way, denying the inevitable persecution toward Bible-believing Christians will not diminish the reality. Paul and the early disciples experienced it. Even so, Paul rejoiced that he was "…not crushed…not driven to despair… never abandoned by God [and] …not destroyed."[56]

God's plan for Paul is God's plan for us.

Some people think, "But God would never do that to me!"

If it's in the Book, one way or another, it's in the script, and therefore it's on the schedule.

Feeling ill prepared to face the monumental tests ahead does

---

[55] 2Corinthians 4:8–9

[56] Ibid.

> **If it's in the Book, one way or another, it's in the script, and therefore it's on the schedule.**

not mean they aren't coming! This is one of the primary reasons God provides prophetic insight: we are able to get ready for what He decrees unavoidable.

Today's tests prepare us for the greater trials of tomorrow.

Even if God doesn't seem to show up; even if our dreams don't come true; even if nothing seems to work out and all our hopes are dashed, He is still worthy of our trust! "Then Christ will make His home in your hearts as you trust in Him. Your roots will grow down into God's love and keep you strong."[57]

When we trust God, demons get whiplash, and angels give high fives! It's been said, half the battle is just showing up.

FLOOD WARNING

Jesus forewarned, "When the rains and floods come and the winds beat against that house, it will collapse with a mighty crash."[58] He didn't say, "It might come." He alerted us to trouble that will attempt to destroy us and those we love.

Readiness is not an option. It is a necessity.

We all want to be loved—even liked. It's not a bad desire unless it conflicts with God's will. There are times, "When people's lives please the LORD, even their enemies are at peace with them."[59] What a joy when this takes place! But on other occasions the psalmist acknowledged conflicts beyond his control saying, "I search for peace; but when I speak of peace, they want war!"[60]

---

57 Ephesians 3:17
58 Matthew 7:27
59 Proverbs 16:7
60 Psalm 120:7

Jesus knows that some of our best intentions, motives and deeds won't be able to remove attitudes of deception, hatred and anger. He alerts us to this reality by encouraging us to prepare: "If the world hates you, remember that it hated Me first. The world would love you as one of its own if you belonged to it, but you are no longer part of the world. I chose you to come out of the world, so it hates you."[61]

Whether we like it or not, we will at times be hated, persecuted, and even killed.

This reality has been true since the crucifixion of Jesus and the martyrdom of almost all of His first disciples. Church history records the fate of those closest to Jesus:

- Matthew was martyred in Ethiopia.
- Mark was dragged through the streets in Egypt.
- Luke was hung in Greece.
- Peter was crucified upside down at Rome.
- James the Great was beheaded at Jerusalem.
- James the less was thrown from pinnacle of the temple.
- Philip was hung.
- Bartholomew was flogged alive.
- Simeon the Zealot and Andrew were both crucified.
- Thomas was pierced with a lance in the East Indies.
- Jude was shot to death with arrows.
- Barnabas and Mathias were stoned.
- Paul the Apostle was beheaded at Rome.

---

[61] John 15:18–19

> **It is estimated that literally millions of Christians have been martyred for their faith since the first century.**

Only John, of the original 11 was not martyred.

It is estimated that literally millions of Christians have been martyred for their faith since the first century.

Paul, the martyred apostle, wrote just prior to his beheading, "Yes, and everyone who wants to live a godly life in Christ Jesus will suffer persecution."[62] I was always puzzled by the fact that he said "everyone." It ends the suspense, as to whom. The only realistic option left is for us to accept what we once thought completely unacceptable.

In the Parable of the Sower, Jesus prepares us for persecution. He said, "The seed on the rocky soil represents those who hear the message and immediately receive it with joy. But since they don't have deep roots, they don't last long. They fall away as soon as they have problems or are persecuted for believing God's word."[63]

Going deep in God is not an option.

It's not an incidental car accessory—it's an essential part of the engine.

When the End Time "great falling away" strikes in full force,[64] the ill-equipped will first face an inner battle. Soldiers drill for the inevitable combat; firefighters train for the inescapable fire, we, as "Bible-believing" Christians, must prepare for inexorable persecution.

Are you in training, or in denial?

Are you preparing, or rationalizing?

A storm of unprecedented proportions lurks on the horizon.

---

62 2Timothy 3:12
63 Matthew 13:20–21
64 2Thessalonians 2:3, NKJV

Are you ready for it?

Jesus again urged, "You also must be ready all the time, for the Son of Man will come when least expected."[65]

As I have pondered this stretching verse over many years, my conclusion is that I am most discouraged, distracted or deceived when I am least expectant. Therefore, I especially shake myself during times of complacency and temptation. I do not want to realize too little too late that I missed the most significant hour of my life.

"Awake, O sleeper, rise up from the dead, and Christ will give you light."[66]

Soldiers drill for the inevitable combat; firefighters train for the inescapable fire, we, as "Bible-believing" Christians, must prepare for inexorable persecution.

TRUE MARTYRS IN A FALSE AGE

It is not coincidental that the selfless, Christ-like love of heaven's true martyrs is now called into question as hell's counterfeits raise their hateful heads.

Suicide bombers, esteemed by those who serve a god who demands innocent life, have polluted the planet with countless murders.

In stark contrast, God's true martyrs reject senseless violence. They serve a God who is love, not hate. A winning view to the Christian faith sees Christ's followers loving those who are killing them. No surprise that this extraordinary sacrificial love was first modeled by our Savior. Paul the Apostle unveiled a comparable willingness when he wrote, "For to me, living means living for Christ, and dying is even better."[67] We don't need to initiate it, but we must not live to avoid it.

---

[65] Matthew 24:44, Luke 12:40

[66] Ephesians 5:14

[67] Philippians 1:21

No scripture describes the disparity between martyrs from Heaven with those from Hell better than the words of Jesus: "The thief's purpose is to steal and kill and destroy. My purpose is to give them a rich and satisfying life."[68] The devil's plan is to senselessly steal, kill and destroy, and then market such crimes against humanity as Heaven's idea. These despicable atrocities bear no resemblance to the selfless acts of authentic Christians and the compassionate God they represent.

Christian martyrs' only crime is that they were sharing the hope found in Christ with a dying world. Subject to torment and death merely because they believed Jesus, they perfectly fulfilled the scriptural admonition: "…that no one pays back evil for evil, but always try to do good to each other and to all people."[69]

What fails to receive justice in this world, will be made right in the next. The Bible affirms this fact with contrasting verses:

"Woe to those who call evil good, and good evil; who put darkness for light, and light for darkness"[70]

"…And we have a priceless inheritance—an inheritance that is kept in Heaven for you, pure and undefiled, beyond the reach of change and decay."[71]

Justice lost on Earth will be found in Heaven.

---

[68] John 10:10b

[69] 1Thessalonians 5:15

[70] Isaiah 5:20

[71] 1Peter 1:4

PANDEMIC PERSECUTION

In 2008, I received an urgent prayer request from Chip and Sandy Wanner, Youth With a Mission (YWAM) missionaries living in Orissa, India. Their startling email foreshadows tumultuous times ahead. Excerpts from their email describe the staggering challenges they were facing in November 2008.

> *"We have never seen anything like this. We knew that Orissa was the most resistant and hostile State in India toward the Gospel. And we brushed off the continuous threats and harassment we faced as we went about His work. But none of our staff imagined that they would see this kind of carnage.... A militant Hindu priest and 4 of his attendants, who were zealously "reconverting" villagers back to Hinduism, were gunned down by unknown assailants in Central Orissa last weekend.*
>
> *"Immediately the cry rose up, 'Kill the Christians!' And the horror began. We have first-hand witnesses to hundreds of churches being blown up or burned and to many, many dozens of Christian tribes being slaughtered. This for no other reason than that they bear the name of Christ.*
>
> *"Night and day I have been in touch with our Good News India Directors spread across 14 Dream Centers in Orissa. They are right in the middle of all this chaos. In Tihidi, just after the police came to offer protection, a group of 70 bloodthirsty militants arrived to kill our staff and destroy the home. They were not allowed in, but they damaged our Dream Center by throwing rocks and bricks and smashing our gate, etc. They have promised to come back and 'finish the job.' Our kids and staff remain locked inside and have stayed that way with doors and windows shut for the past 3 days. It has been a time of desperately calling on the Lord in prayer. More police have come to offer protection.*

"In Kalahandi, the police and some local sympathizers, in an effort to help, gave our staff and kids about three minutes notice to vacate. No one had time to even grab a change of clothes or any personal belongings. As they fled, the mob came to kill everyone in the building. We would have had a mass funeral there, but for His grace.

"In Phulbani, the mob came looking for Christian homes and missions. The local Hindu people, our neighbors, turned them away by saying that there were no Christians in the area. So they left.. We had favor. The same thing happened in Balasore.

"Our kids and staff are huddled inside the dream centers while police patrol the outside. The fanatics are circling the perimeter waiting for a chance to kill. Others were not so fortunate. In a nearby Catholic orphanage, the mob allowed the kids to leave but locked up a Priest and a computer teacher and burned them to death.

"Many believers have been killed, hacked to pieces and left on the road... even women and children. Under attack, the director and his wife of another orphanage jumped on their motorbike and simply fled, leaving all the children and staff behind.

"Every one of our GNI directors that I have spoken to said: 'We stay with our kids...we live together or die together, but we will never abandon what God has called us to do.' More than 5,000 Christian families have had their homes burned or destroyed. They have fled into the jungles and are living in great fear waiting for the authorities to bring about peace. But so far, no peace is foreseen. This will continue for another ten days...supposedly the 14-day mourning period for the slain Hindu priest.

> "Many more Christians will die and their houses destroyed. Many more churches will be smashed down. The federal government is trying to restore order and perhaps things will calm down. We ask for your prayers. Only the hand of God can calm this storm. None of us knew the meaning of persecution. But now our kids and staff know. So many of our kids coming from Hindu backgrounds are totally bewildered at what is happening around them.
>
> "So many of their guardians have fled into the jungles and are unable to protect them during these trying times. Through all this, I am more determined than ever to continue with our goal: the transformation of a community through the transformation of its children. Orissa will be saved...that is our hearts' cry. If we can rescue these thousands of throwaway children and help them become disciples of Jesus, they will transform an entire region. It is a long-term goal, but it is strategic thinking in terms of the Great Commission."

Chip and Sandy then closed their email by asking for fervent prayer.

In the Western media, the events just described went completely unreported. Had those victims been members of the homosexual community, or if they were abortion clinics, outrage would have echoed around the world. But Christians and unborn babies have always been fair game in a world where pleasure and self-gratification top the agenda.

Christians and unborn babies have always been fair game in a world where pleasure and self-gratification top the agenda.

In the years ahead, many comparable situations involving Christians will occur—even in the Western World. We must be ready for what will surely come.

The Apostle Peter understood the reality and inevitability of persecution when he wrote, "So then, since Christ suffered physical pain, you must arm yourselves with the same attitude He had, and be ready to suffer, too. For if you have suffered physically for Christ, you have finished with sin. Dear friends, don't be surprised at the fiery trials you are going through, as if something strange were happening to you. Instead, be very glad—for these trials make you partners with Christ in His suffering, so that you will have the wonderful joy of seeing His glory when it is revealed to all the world. So be happy when you are insulted for being a Christian, for then the glorious Spirit of God rests upon you. If you suffer, however, it must not be for murder, stealing, making trouble, or prying into other people's affairs. But it is no shame to suffer for being a Christian. Praise God for the privilege of being called by His name! For the time has come for judgment, and it must begin with God's household. And if judgment begins with us, what terrible fate awaits those who have never obeyed God's Good News? And also, 'If the righteous are barely saved, what will happen to godless sinners?'"[72]

This was not a first century admonition.

This warns all who read and believe it.

May we have the faith to believe, trust and endure in this our day.

---

[72] 1Peter 4:1, 12–18

QUESTIONS FOR DISCUSSION

1. What is your greatest concern about the future? Have you considered praying about this? If so, in what ways has it affected you?

2. Did you ever ridicule Christians before you became a follower of Jesus? If so, how did that ridicule affect the Christians? How did it affect you?

3. Have you ever been persecuted for your faith in Jesus? What did this look like? How did you respond? How did your response affect others and yourself?

4. Is your heart prepared to "…love your enemies, pray for those who persecute you…"[73] and "…bless those who curse you"?[74] If not, in what ways could you begin to prepare your heart?

5. Would you still stand for Jesus if it cost your life, and/or the lives of those you love? Contemplate what would influence your decision.

---

[73] Matthew 5:44

[74] Luke 6:28

9 ETERNAL CHURCH
CHAPTER NINE

> "We have learned that there is a City of God: and we have longed to become citizens of that City with a love inspired by its Founder."
>
> **AUGUSTINE**[1]

When Heaven meets Earth, they won't be strangers.

Having dreamt of one another since the beginning of time, their joining will be a completion, not an introduction.

Just as a true prophecy from God often confirms what is already planted in our hearts, so being in the presence of God will confirm what we intuitively know: that Heaven belongs on Earth.

When Jesus prayed to His Father in Heaven, "May Your Kingdom come soon. May Your will be done on earth, as it is in heaven,"[2] it wasn't wishful thinking. It was affirming His mission.

He came to bring Heaven to Earth.

All of Heaven yearns for this to happen. Likewise, all of conscious Earth longs for the same. Much of Earth lies

---

1 Dyson RW. *Augustine: The City of God Against the Pagan.* Cambridge Texts in the History of Political Thought (Cambridge University Press, 1998).

2 Matthew 6:10

> **From the moment Earth fell into rebellion and became separated from her Heavenly Creator, the focus of all existence has been a rescue mission.**

asleep, unaware of her true calling and purpose. But when she awakes, she will live like she was created to live.

From the moment Earth fell into rebellion and became separated from her Heavenly Creator, the focus of all existence has been a rescue mission. God the Father's finale will unite His perfect Son with His transformed Bride: perfect Heaven with restored Earth. Christian theologian, Anthony Hoekema, states that "we must see [history] as moving toward the goal of a finally restored and glorified universe."

"Then the seventh angel blew his trumpet, and there were loud voices shouting in heaven: 'The world has now become the Kingdom of our Lord and of His Christ, and He will reign forever and ever.'"[3]

John describes this happiest of all endings in this way: "Then I saw a new heaven and a new earth, for the old heaven and the old earth had disappeared. And the sea was also gone. And I saw the holy city, the new Jerusalem, coming down from God out of heaven like a bride beautifully dressed for her husband. I heard a loud shout from the throne, saying, 'Look, God's home is now among His people! He will live with them, and they will be His people. God Himself will be with them. He will wipe every tear from their eyes, and there will be no more death or sorrow or crying or pain. All these things are gone forever.'"[4]

The greatest, grandest shout will emanate from Heaven when it is at last united with the Earth God loves. Till then we groan in anticipation of that glorious day. What else can we do?

We are starving for Heaven!

---

[3] Revelation 11:15

[4] Revelation 21:3b-4

The Bible confirms this:

> "For all creation is waiting eagerly for that future day when God will reveal who His children really are. Against its will, all creation was subjected to God's curse. But with eager hope, creation looks forward to the day when it will join God's children in glorious freedom from death and decay. For we know that all creation has been groaning as in the pains of childbirth right up to the present time. And we believers also groan, even though we have the Holy Spirit within us as a foretaste of future glory, for we long for our bodies to be released from sin and suffering. We, too, wait with eager hope for the day when God will give us our full rights as his adopted children, including the new bodies He has promised us. We were given this hope when we were saved. (If we already have something, we don't need to hope for it. But if we look forward to something we don't yet have, we must wait patiently and confidently.)"[5]

THE CHURCH: CHRIST'S BRIDE

From eternity past, our Heavenly Father's great longing has been to prepare a bride for His Son. First, the Son made Himself ready passing the test of Earth. Now it is the brides turn.

Christ will return for "…a glorious church without a spot or wrinkle or any other blemish. Instead, she will be holy and without fault."[6] It will be a great and glorious celebration! "Let us be glad and rejoice, and let us give honor to Him. For the time has come for the wedding feast of the Lamb, and His bride has prepared herself."[7]

> **First, the Son made Himself ready passing the test of Earth. Now it is the brides turn.**

---

[5] Romans 8:19–25

[6] Ephesians 5:27

[7] Revelation 19:7

Jesus longs to be united with His beautiful bride. "You have made my heart beat faster, my sister, my bride; you have made my heart beat faster with a single glance of your eyes."[8]

Before this glorious wedding can occur, God's bride will be drawn into the inner chambers of His heart. "Draw me away! We will run after you. The king has brought me into his chambers. We will be glad and rejoice in you. We will remember your love more than wine."[9]

If we respond to His leadings, intimacy with our Creator awaits us. If not, we will miss the opportunity of a lifetime to know and be known by the One who loves us most.

In the parable Jesus told of the ten virgins or bridesmaids, five had lamps supplied with oil and five did not. At midnight, as the bridegroom approached, the five foolish virgins begged the wise virgins for oil. As Jesus recounts the story, "...the others replied, 'We don't have enough for all of us. Go to a shop and buy some for yourselves.' But while they were gone to buy oil, the bridegroom came. Then those who were ready went in with Him to the marriage feast, and the door was locked. Later, when the other five bridesmaids returned, they stood outside, calling, 'Lord! Lord! Open the door for us!' But He called back, 'Believe Me, I don't know you!' So you, too, must keep watch! For you do not know the day or hour of My return."[10]

Jesus challenges us to, "Watch and pray!"[11] and warns, "Look, I will come as unexpectedly as a thief! Blessed are all who are watching for Me, who keep their clothing ready so they will not have to walk around naked and ashamed."[12]

---

[8] Song of Solomon 4:9, NASB

[9] Song 1:4, NKJV

[10] Matthew 25:9–13

[11] Matthew 26:41, Mark 13:33

[12] Revelation 16:15

Deep within, we each yearn for the day when we join the One our heart was made for. "He brought me to the banqueting house, and His banner over me was love...for I am lovesick."[13]

THE CHURCH OF HIS DREAMS

He waits nervously at the altar, uncomfortable in his tuxedo, but exhilarated at the prospect of the vision in white that will appear soon. He is madly in love with his bride, longing for her and no one else. Having resisted the temptation of other lovers, he has kept himself for her alone, the fulfillment of his desires, the dream of his dreams.

If we can imagine this, we will catch a glimpse of how much Jesus is longing to be with His Bride, and Heaven is pining to be united with Earth. When the true Church of Jesus Christ fully embraces her matchless identity and unsurpassed destiny, she will at long last become the authentic, accepting, transparent, discerning, and supernatural Bride God created from the depths of His endless imagination.

God is the most authentic, accepting, transparent, discerning, and supernatural Person who ever lived.

Not limited to His Church on Earth, these five qualities already subsist in Heaven, and for one truly remarkable reason: they represent the nature of God. Though it seems almost trite to write: God is the most authentic, accepting, transparent, discerning, and supernatural Person who ever lived. And He created us, not just to be with Him, but also to be like Him.

In eternity past, "...God said, 'Let us make human beings in our image, to be like ourselves.'"[14] Out of all God's creation, only humans share God's likeness. The Bible does not say that animals or even angels have been given this privilege...only mankind.

---

13 Song of Solomon 2:4, 5b, NKJV

14 Genesis 1:26a

Animals own no personalities, no capacity to accumulate knowledge. In their limited state, they are unable to experience emotions such as love or hate. They have no conscience, nor possess the ability to make moral decisions. Lastly, and most importantly, animals are without a spirit, and therefore cannot commune with their Creator.

As Heaven perfectly represents the majestic dimensions of God, so too His perfected Bride will personify His attributes as well. Truly, Jesus and His Bride are the original match made in Heaven.

As God's Church embodies what is most valued by her Creator, the test of Earth will be complete. Heaven will come for His church. At that momentous time, the greatest cheer will erupt from the corridors of eternity.

At long last this verse will be fulfilled, "Then I heard again what sounded like the shout of a vast crowd or the roar of mighty ocean waves or the crash of loud thunder: 'Praise the LORD! For the Lord our God, the Almighty, reigns. Let us be glad and rejoice, and let us give honor to Him. For the time has come for the wedding feast of the Lamb, and His bride has prepared herself. She has been given the finest of pure white linen to wear.' For the fine linen represents the good deeds of God's holy people."[15]

As we have discussed, a prepared Church, ready to meet her heavenly Bridegroom, will model five qualities found first in God the creator.

He is authentic, accepting, transparent, discerning and supernatural.

---

[15] Revelation 19:6-8

THE AUTHENTIC GOD

God is the source of all that exists, the very definition of authentic. There are no copies of God, no duplicates. He is the only truly original Person in the Universe. There can only be one First and one Last; one Beginning and one End; one Alpha and one Omega.[16] He is the One-of-a-kind Creator of all that is, or ever will be.

Jesus, God the Son, likewise shares this marvelous quality with His Father. The Bible says, "Christ is the visible image of the invisible God. He existed before anything was created and is supreme over all creation, for through Him God created everything in the heavenly realms and on earth. He made the things we can see and the things we can't see—such as thrones, kingdoms, rulers, and authorities in the unseen world. Everything was created through Him and for Him. He existed before anything else, and he holds all creation together."[17]

> **Heaven is all it claims to be. No locks, no alarms, no fear—all is safe, beyond harm or decay.**

If God was in some way not who He says He is, if there was any dishonesty or duplicity in His person, He would not be worthy of our worship, our trust, nor our love and admiration. Yet, God alone is true. "Whatever is good and perfect comes down to us from God our Father, who created all the lights in the heavens. He never changes or casts a shifting shadow."[18]

Perhaps, for this reason, we respect integrity most when we see it in others. It is most modeled in Heaven. Without unreality or disingenuousness, Heaven is all it claims to be. No locks, no alarms, no fear—all is safe, beyond harm or decay. We were created to thrive in this absolutely peaceful place.

---

16 Revelation 22:13

17 Colossians 1:15–17

18 James 1:17

The absence of Heaven generates an atmosphere of fear, doubt, unbelief, distrust, disconnect, and even hate. If I know and trust someone, then I can rest and enjoy him. If, on the other hand, I question a person's motive or honesty, my guard raises, and frankly, I do not want to be around him. Lack of integrity ruins relationships, destroys trust and, as we said in chapter two, misrepresents the God who is Truth.

For now, I must bring Heaven with me because most places on Earth are void of any replication of Heaven. If I don't bring it, it almost never meets me. Jesus promised that if we yield our life to Him, then "…the kingdom of God is within you."[19]

Someone claiming to represent the Kingdom of God that, in reality, does not, disappoints beyond measure. The prophet Isaiah warned, "But watch out, you who live in your own light and warm yourselves by your own fires. This is the reward you will receive from Me: You will soon fall down in great torment."[20]

A counterfeit representation of God on Earth is a crime against Heaven.

Better to wear prison chains and abide in truth, than to cruise the world living a lie. Our greatest regrets will always have to do with our not being who we should be. This is why James, the Lord's brother, affirms that God blesses the person who looks into His Word, "…the perfect law that sets you free…" if he does what it says and doesn't forget.[21]

May we not forget who we are, and from Whom we came. Only then can we live the authentic life God intended for us. "…God chose you to be the holy people He loves, you must clothe yourselves with tenderhearted mercy, kindness, humility, gentleness, and patience."[22]

---

[19] Luke 17:21b, NKJV

[20] Isaiah 50:11

[21] James 1:25

[22] Colossians 3:12

THE ACCEPTING GOD

In the beginning of 2009, two older men who had been in the homosexual lifestyle since their youth stood before our congregation to share their testimony. They had been coming to our church for less than a year, being totally loved and accepted by all. One of them in his own words said, "I have Jesus in my life. Through the love that has been shown to me here, my old life style is gone. No more bars, no more temptations. Since finding the Lord, my relationship of 20 years has changed from a life of sexual gratuity to one of deep friendship, knowing each other the way the Lord intended."

There is nothing more fulfilling than watching the accepting God work through His accepting people.

God's acceptance is based on absolute fairness.

No one does "fair" like God.

He shows no favoritism; no partiality.[23] He loves everyone equally.

When Jesus encouraged His followers to love their enemies, He promised, if they did, they would be like His Father. "In that way, you will be acting as true children of your Father in heaven. For He gives His sunlight to both the evil and the good, and He sends rain on the just and the unjust alike."[24]

There is nothing more fulfilling than watching the accepting God work through His accepting people.

Jesus is saying, My Father is so impartial and without prejudice that He treats all of His creation fairly. No intolerance or bias exists in Heaven. No one will ever feel cheated or shortchanged. God the Father is not just fair with those who love Him, but equally with those who hate Him. "If God were not entirely fair, how would He be qualified to judge the world?"[25]

---

23 Acts 10:34, NLT-SE, NKJV
24 Matthew 5:45
25 Romans 3:6b

"He is the Rock; His deeds are perfect. Everything He does is just and fair. He is a faithful God who does no wrong; how just and upright He is!"[26]

Only God knows how good good is. God not only protects pure love, just treatment, and right behaviors, but He willingly forgives those who break His established laws.

God led the rescue mission Himself, choosing, out of all possible options—the one that would cost Him the most, the one that would allow every crime against Him to be forgiven.

"For God presented Jesus as the sacrifice for sin. People are made right with God when they believe that Jesus sacrificed His life, shedding His blood. This sacrifice shows that God was being fair when He held back and did not punish those who sinned in times past, for He was looking ahead and including them in what He would do in this present time. God did this to demonstrate His righteousness, for He Himself is fair and just, and He declares sinners to be right in His sight when they believe in Jesus."[27]

No one is more accepting than God. Those who think they are, upon closer examination, will realize they have compromised what is eternal for what was merely temporal—exchanging the memorable for the immediate.

How do we know we have God's heart for others? When we unconditionally love and accept people, while courageously protecting goodness and holiness.

The God of love can rescue us whenever we are willing to exchange our flawed whims for His flawless plan.

---

26 Deuteronomy 32:4

27 Romans 3:25-26

THE TRANSPARENT GOD

As God desires Earth to reflect Heaven, He longs for Christians to reflect Jesus.

The Book of Revelation gives us a glimpse of Heaven: "In front of the throne [of God] was a shiny sea of glass [transparent like rain], sparkling like crystal."[28] This is the picture of a transparent God, fully revealed, sitting upon a transparent throne looking out across a sea of glass, transparent like rain.

In vivid detail, the Bible describes what surrounds God's throne: "In the center and around the throne were four living beings, each covered with eyes, front and back."[29] I would assume that beings who have eyes looking in every direction would know what is going on. You could say they're not missing much.

The Book of Revelation also says, "...the holy city, Jerusalem, descending out of Heaven from God...shone with the glory of God and sparkled like a precious stone—like jasper as clear as crystal."[30] The word "crystal" comes from the Greek *krustallizo*, which refers to ice or rock crystal.

Heaven is a transparent place where a transparent God dwells. He calls His bride to be visible and transparent not just before Him, but also before those He loves on Earth.

Heaven is a transparent place where a transparent God dwells. He calls His bride to be visible and transparent not just before Him, but also before those He loves on Earth.

John the Apostle described it further in his vision: "Then the angel showed me a river with the water of life, clear as crystal, flowing from the throne of God and of the Lamb."[31]

---

28 Revelation 4:6a
29 Revelation 4:6b
30 Revelation 21:10–11
31 Revelation 22:1

"The construction of its wall was of jasper, and the city was pure gold, as clear as glass [transparent like rain]."[32]

The Bible says, "The twelve gates were twelve pearls—each gate from a single pearl! And the main street was pure gold, as clear as glass."

From these profoundly revealing verses, we can see all that comes from God is clear as crystal: from His celestial city, to its walls, its streets, and even the water of life that flows like transparent rain—clear as crystal.[33]

So too is God's vulnerable bride!

Though our shame will be covered, the eternal epitaph of our battle scars and their victories will attest to God's glorious grace and gift of salvation. This all sounds absolutely breathtaking, but what are the implications of this kind of Heaven coming to Earth?

Perhaps Jesus gives us a key to the mystery.

Jesus said:

> *"No one, when he has lit a lamp, puts it in a secret place or under a basket, but on a lamp stand, that those who come in may see the light. The lamp of the body is the eye. Therefore, when your eye is good, your whole body also is full of light [lustrous, bright, transparent or well-illuminated]. But when your eye is bad, your body also is full of darkness [opaque or impervious to light, so that images cannot be seen through it]. Therefore take heed that the light [the fire] which is in you is not darkness [shadiness]. If then your whole body is full of light, having no part dark, the whole body will be full of light [lustrous, bright, transparent or well-illuminated], as when the bright shining of a lamp gives you light."*[34]

---

[32] Revelation 21:18

[33] Revelation 21:21

[34] Luke 11:33–36, NKJV (Emphasis mine.)

A careful exegesis of these verses reveals one dimension of what I believe the Bible is saying: What Jesus has done in us, for us, and to us is the essence of our personal testimony. Lives that are shrouded in darkness are impervious to the light of God. We cannot see through into them. Who they really are and are meant to be has been hidden. A shadiness keeps the true person from being revealed.

On the other hand, lives that please God are simultaneously bright and transparent. Those who truly represent their Father in Heaven, who allow Heaven to come to Earth in them, live lives for all to see. Jesus in us is our testimony.

Jesus came from light, is light, and returned to light. He did not hide the truth. He was and is the Truth. While on Earth, He said what He meant and meant what He said, confessing that "…in secret I have said nothing."[35]

The words of Jesus fittingly summarize this section: "The time is coming when everything that is covered up will be revealed, and all that is secret will be made known to all. Whatever you have said in the dark will be heard in the light, and what you have whispered behind closed doors will be shouted from the housetops for all to hear!"[36]

May we willingly allow all that has been accomplished in us and for us to shine for others to see.

---

35 John 18:20b, NKJV

36 Luke 12:2–3

THE DISCERNING GOD

We are the ultimate fulfillment of God's creative imagination. He wasn't on the sideline watching; He was in the forefront. Before the foundation of the world He knew us; not just facts and knowledge, but identity and destiny; not just personality and temperament, but gifting and calling; not just what we could be, but what we would be. Nevertheless, He will never use His absolute knowledge to manipulate, but rather to guide and inspire.

God alone has discerned the premier purpose for our lives. Only through His Holy Spirit are we able to discern it.

What have we created that is eternal? What do we know of perfect purity—and selfless intention? Have we ever known, not just every thought others have had, but the actual motives behind each thought? Until we can answer these questions with the capacity of a loving Creator, we should humbly acknowledge that they are out of our league.

God alone has discerned the premier purpose for our lives. Only through His Holy Spirit are we able to discern it.

Without freedom to choose, true love is not possible. Choosing to receive His love, to trust Him in our darkest hour, blesses Him most. As the Everlasting Father,[37] He longs to fulfill our lives. As a determined Lover, He will not waver until our hearts join as one.

In the original Greek language, Christ's prayer, "May Your Kingdom come soon. May Your will be done on earth, as it is in heaven,"[38] speaks of the Father's purpose, determination, decree, desire, and pleasure to fulfill His will. It matches God's best for us. He has already thought through every possible scenario, and chosen the finest option.

---

37 Isaiah 9:6

38 Matthew 6:10

This premier purpose is His will.

To receive His best, simply use what He has given. Take note of an immutable fact: "it is impossible to please God without faith. Anyone who wants to come to Him must believe that God exists and that He rewards those who sincerely seek Him."[39]

Faith guarantees all that we have been hardwired to hope for. It will not disappoint. "Now faith is the substance (the assurance) of things hoped for, the evidence of things not seen."[40]

Faith necessitates a firm trust. Without trust there can be little faith. Faith is confident in the character of the trusted. It tests and proves trustworthiness.

We can rest in faith; enjoy the ride; watch the scenery; knowing implicitly that because God is behind the wheel, we will arrive at the best of all destinations. It is only when we lack discernment that we fail to fully trust the God who has already discerned.

As His beloved sons and daughters, we have complete access to the only Person who knows the outcome. He is not the variable; we are. He is the constant, worthy of our complete trust and confidence. That is why God delights when we trust His motive for us.

For this reason the Bible says "…He brings His reward with Him as He comes."[41] He comes to bless. He comes to satisfy. Let your heart trust who He says He is and what He says He will do.[42]

---

[39] Hebrews 11:6

[40] Hebrews 11:1, NKJV

[41] Isaiah 62:11b

[42] Hebrews 11:6

THE SUPERNATURAL GOD

Since the beginning of creation, mankind has been natural and supernatural, spiritual and physical. When God finally fashions the New Heaven and the New Earth,[43] the natural and supernatural and the spiritual and physical realms will join. Notice a sequence here.

We ache for more. This acute longing presses beyond the natural canopy of Earth into our full inheritance.

Genesis recounts that God created Adam first physically. Then He breathed into him a spirit. "The first man, Adam, became a living person."[44] But the last Adam—that is, Christ—is a life-giving Spirit. What comes first is the natural body. The spiritual body comes later.

Adam, the first man, was made from the dust of the earth, while Christ, the second man, came from heaven. Earthly people are like the earthly man, and heavenly people are like the heavenly man. Just as we are now like the earthly man, we will someday be like the heavenly man."[45]

While on Earth, in this present dispensation, we straddle two dimensions: the natural and supernatural. Our capacity to traverse between these two realities parallels the future seamless unity of Heaven and Earth. We ache for more. This acute longing presses beyond the natural canopy of Earth into our full inheritance: the complete supernatural man and woman, functioning on all cylinders, flowing in the fullness of our persona.

When Heaven and Earth are at last forged into one, it will be very much like the joining of Christ and His Church: "This is a great mystery, but it is an illustration of the way Christ and the church are one."[46] The wedding of Christ and His bride joins

---

43 Revelation 21:1

44 Genesis 2:7b

45 1Corinthians 15:45–49

46 Ephesians 5:32

two realms: natural and spiritual, physical and supernatural. "And this is the plan: At the right time He will bring everything together under the authority of Christ—everything in heaven and on earth."[47]

This Wedding is also a welding where two become One. The original intention is fulfilled. "Heaven is God's home. Earth is our home. Jesus Christ, as the God-man, forever links God and mankind, and thereby forever links Heaven and Earth. As Ephesians 1:10 demonstrates, this idea of Earth and Heaven becoming one is explicitly biblical. Christ will make Earth into Heaven and Heaven into Earth."[48]

PERFECTION REFLECTION

The Bible says that Earth is in some way a replica of Heaven.

"That is why the Tabernacle and everything in it, which were copies of things in heaven, had to be purified by the blood of animals. But the real things in heaven had to be purified with far better sacrifices than the blood of animals. For Christ did not enter into a holy place made with human hands, which was only a copy of the true one in heaven. He entered into heaven itself to appear now before God on our behalf."[49]

From these verses it seems that just as God created humans in His own image,[50] He created the Earth in the image of Heaven, and not the other way around.

C.S. Lewis suggests that, "the hills and valleys of Heaven will be to those you now experience not as a copy is to an original, nor as a substitute is to the genuine article, but as the flower to the root, or the diamond to the coal."

---

[47] Ephesians 1:10

[48] Alcorn R. *Heaven* (Tyndale House Publishers, 2004).

[49] Hebrews 9:23–24 (Emphasis mine.)

[50] Genesis 1:27

As God redeems our old lives, He also redeems all aspects of creation.

In a thorough study of Heaven, Randy Alcorn writes, "Often our thinking is backwards. Why do we imagine that God patterns Heaven's holy city after an earthly city, as if Heaven knows nothing of community and culture and has to get its ideas from us? Isn't it more likely that earthly realities, including cities, are derived from heavenly counterparts? We tend to start with Earth and reason up toward Heaven, when instead we should start with Heaven and reason down toward Earth."[51]

Insight into the relationship of the Eternal Church with the New Heaven and New Earth can be seen throughout the Old Heaven and Old Earth. Jesus prayed for God's will to be done on Earth as it is in Heaven.[52]

Evidence of Heaven already exists on the Old Earth. "If we can't imagine our present Earth without rivers, mountains, trees, and flowers, then why would we try to imagine the New Earth without these features? We wouldn't expect a non-Earth to have mountains and rivers. But God doesn't promise us a non-Earth. He promises us a New Earth."[53]

God never intended to start from scratch in any eternal dimension. As God redeems our old lives, He also redeems all aspects of creation. "God has never given up on His original creation. Yet somehow we've managed to overlook an entire biblical vocabulary that makes this point clear. Reconcile. Redeem. Restore. Recover. Return. Renew. Regenerate. Resurrect. Redemption means to buy back what was formerly owned. Similarly, reconciliation means the restoration or reestablishment of a prior friendship or unity. Renewal means to make new again, restoring to an original state. Resurrection means becoming physically alive again, after death."[54]

---

51 Alcorn R. *Heaven* (Tyndale House Publishers, 2004).

52 Matthew 6:10

53 Alcorn R. *Heaven* (Tyndale House Publishers, 2004).

54 Ibid.

I have seen in my own life, years of ambiguity fully redeemed in a moment's time. "The earthly beauty we now see won't be lost. We won't trade Earth's beauty for Heaven's but retain Earth's beauty and gain even deeper beauty. As we will live forever with the people of this world—redeemed—we will enjoy forever the beauties of this world—redeemed."[55]

But what will this New Heaven be like?

The Book of Revelation provides some detail: "The angel who talked to me held in his hand a gold measuring stick to measure the city, its gates, and its wall. When he measured it, he found it was a square, as wide as it was long. In fact, its length and width and height were each 1,400 miles."[56]

Randy Alcorn elaborates, "Fifteen times in Revelation 21 and 22 the place God and His people will live together is called a city. The city at the center of the future Heaven is called the New Jerusalem. The city's exact dimensions are measured by an angel and reported to be the equivalent of 1,400 miles in length, width, and height."[57]

Some commentators have embellished the biblical narrative of Heaven based upon the original language. William Hendriksen suggests, "The term 'tree of life' is collective,[58] just like 'avenue' and 'river.' The idea is not that there is just one single tree. No, there is an entire park: whole rows of trees alongside the river; hence, between the river and the avenue. And this is true with respect to all the avenues of the city. Hence, the city is just full of parks. Observe, therefore, this wonderful truth: the city is full of rivers of life. It is also full of parks containing trees of life. These trees, moreover, are full of fruit."

Obviously, the real Heaven will be infinitely grander than anything we can either describe or comprehend on this side

---

[55] Alcorn R. *Heaven* (Tyndale House Publishers, 2004).

[56] Revelation 21:15–16

[57] Alcorn R. *Heaven* (Tyndale House Publishers, 2004).

[58] Revelation 2:7

of eternity. But how marvelous it is to imagine! The Book of Revelation affords a breath-taking snapshot of the celebration awaiting us in the New Heaven and Earth. "After this I saw a vast crowd, too great to count, from every nation and tribe and people and language, standing in front of the throne and before the Lamb. They were clothed in white robes and held palm branches in their hands."[59]

At last, the Bride of Christ will be made ready, and the oneness that we have longed for on Earth will at last be realized. Till then, consigned to drive through the thick forest of Old Earth, we occasionally catch a glimpse of eternal wonder through the trees.

TWO JUDGMENTS

Two judgments await us in eternity.

The first is the Judgment of Faith. Dependent not on our works but on our faith in Jesus Christ, it will determine whether I spend eternity in Heaven or Hell. It is not based upon what we have done for God, but upon whether we have received what He did for us.

If we received God's saving grace, then when God judges us, He sees His Son's sacrifice, and not our sin. The Bible says, "God saved you by His grace when you believed. And you can't take credit for this; it is a gift from God. Salvation is not a reward for the good things we have done, so none of us can boast about it."[60]

The Book of Titus adds, "He saved us, not because of the righteous things we had done, but because of His mercy. He washed away our sins, giving us a new birth and new life through the Holy Spirit."[61]

---

59 Revelation 7:9

60 Ephesians 2:8–9

61 Titus 3:5

The second judgment is the Judgment of Works. Our works do not determine our salvation, but they do determine our reward. "...on the Judgment Day, fire will reveal what kind of work each builder has done. The fire will show if a person's work has any value. If the work survives, that builder will receive a reward."[62]

If our motive for doing righteous deeds seeks the attention and applause of others, then we will receive this reward alone. Paul the Apostle further states, "For we must all stand before Christ to be judged. We will each receive whatever we deserve for the good or evil we have done in this earthly body."[63]

Jesus likewise said, "And I tell you this, you must give an account on judgment day for every idle word you speak."[64] It seems apparent from this emphatic sentence that, in the presence of perfection Himself, we will remember and be responsible for far more than we can presently recall. We cannot minimize the significance of this challenging statement. If Jesus said it, He meant it, and if He meant it, we must allow the full scope of His words to have their intended impact. People fritter away their lives in the here and now, often times ignorant of the consequence of their motives, words and deeds.

How significant are our good deeds done with a pure motives?

Our good deeds on Earth epitomize the Bride's wedding dress in Heaven. In eternity, just prior to the Wedding Feast of the Lamb, a large crowd will say: "'Let us be glad and rejoice, and let us give honor to Him. For the time has come for the wedding feast of the Lamb, and His bride has prepared herself.

If Jesus said it, He meant it, and if He meant it, we must allow the full scope of His words to have their intended impact.

---

[62] 1Corinthians 3:13–14

[63] 2Corinthians 5:10

[64] Matthew 12:36

She has been given the finest of pure white linen to wear.' For the fine linen represents the good deeds of God's holy people."[65] Will we spend eternity lamenting our mistakes on Earth? I think not.

As was discussed in chapter four, *Transparent Church*, I believe we will have complete awareness of who we were on Earth: the good, the bad, and the in-between. Yet, in the company of grace personified, we will not experience any guilt, shame, pride or conceit. Likewise, "…there will be no more death or sorrow or crying or pain."[66] Every aspect of the judgment though humbling, will be saturated with the grace and forgiveness of a merciful God.

Proper assessment of ourselves should be as Jesus said, "…when you obey Me you should say, 'We are unworthy servants who have simply done our duty.'"[67] Yet, in the judgment, we long to hear what has been promised: "Well done, good and faithful servant…enter into the joy of your Lord."[68]

One glorious day our King will say: "…Come, you who are blessed by My Father, inherit the Kingdom prepared for you from the creation of the world."[69]

---

65 Revelation 19:7–8

66 Revelation 21:4b

67 Luke 17:10

68 Matthew 25:21, 23, NKJV

69 Matthew 25:34

THE LOVESICK CHURCH

We are made for a person: Jesus.

We have a place to call home: Heaven.

Longing for both isn't wrong. It is God's will. "All praise to God, the Father of our Lord Jesus Christ. It is by His great mercy that we have been born again, because God raised Jesus Christ from the dead. Now we live with great expectation, and we have a priceless inheritance—an inheritance that is kept in heaven for you, pure and undefiled, beyond the reach of change and decay."[70]

We long for our first love, for the One Who loved us first—the same One Who loves us most. We long for the simplicity and intimacy of first love, even its pristine location Eden. The New Heaven and the New Earth must include the New Eden.

Somehow the New Heaven and New Earth will be joined into one, just as Christ and the Church will be made one. "Then I saw a new heaven and a new earth, for the old heaven and the old earth had disappeared. And the sea was also gone. And I saw the holy city, the new Jerusalem, coming down from God out of heaven like a bride beautifully dressed for her husband. I heard a loud shout from the throne, saying, 'Look, God's home is now among His people! He will live with them, and they will be His people. God Himself will be with them.'"[71]

God is the ultimate recycler; nothing is ever wasted. There are no accidents, no coincidences. Everything has its purpose, especially for those who choose to fully trust Him and see their lives from His perspective. "God created Adam and Eve to be king and queen over the Earth. Their job was to rule the Earth, to the glory of God. They failed. Jesus Christ is the second

---

[70] 1Peter 1:3–4

[71] Revelation 21:1–3

Christ is the King, the Church is His queen.

Adam, and the Church is His bride, the second Eve. Christ is the King, the Church is His queen."[72]

Paul's letter to Timothy affirms this call to reign. "If we endure hardship, we will reign with Him. If we deny Him, He will deny us."[73] Again, in the Book of Romans: "And since we are His children, we are His heirs. In fact, together with Christ we are heirs of God's glory. But if we are to share His glory, we must also share His suffering."[74]

"The future heaven is centered more on activity and expansion, serving Christ and reigning with Him… The emphasis in the present heaven is on the absence of earth's negatives, while in the future heaven it is the presence of earth's positives, magnified many times through the power and glory of resurrected bodies on a resurrected earth, free at last from sin and shame and all that would hinder both joy and achievement."[75]

"…in the end, the holy people of the Most High will be given the kingdom, and they will rule forever and ever."[76]

So, what does a God who has everything want?

One thing: US! He created us for Himself.

Being all-powerful and able to choose from all possible options, God created that which would satisfy Him most. Being all wise, He made this the quintessential "win-win" scenario. God is as blessed as we are. He and we will continue to reap the fruit of His marvelous and flawless plan throughout eternity.

---

72 Heaven, Randy Alcorn

73 2Timothy 2:12

74 Romans 8:17

75 René Pache

76 Daniel 7:18

Speaking of this perfect love relationship, the Bible says, "He escorts me to the banquet hall; it's obvious how much he loves me."[77] God has never felt defrauded by this arrangement, expressing with complete contentment, "Your love delights me, my treasure, my bride. Your love is better than wine, your perfume more fragrant than spices."[78]

The lovesick God longs for His Bride to desire Him equally. This is why He lavishes us with His presence, His Word, His promises, and a pristine planet that shadows its future self.

His love letters to us provide a brief look at His heart toward us. "Place me like a seal over your heart, like a seal on your arm. For love is as strong as death, its jealousy as enduring as the grave. Love flashes like fire, the brightest kind of flame. Many waters cannot quench love, nor can rivers drown it. If a man tried to buy love with all his wealth, his offer would be utterly scorned."[79]

Seal us Lord, to Your courts above.
On the other side of our death is God's Living Church.
Her Purpose is to be Authentic.
Her Heart is to be Accepting.
Her Destiny is to be Transparent.
Her Focus is to be Discerning.
Her Vision is to be Supernatural.
Her Voice is to be Virtual.
Though the Battle will increase when she is Persecuted,
Her Future is Eternal and cannot be taken away.

You are that Church.
Live your story.

*Addendum to Chapter 9 found on page 256

---

[77] Song 2:4
[78] Song 4:10
[79] Song 8:6–7

QUESTIONS FOR DISCUSSION

1. Are you 100 percent persuaded that you will spend eternity with Jesus? Why?

2. Do you live each day conscious of eternity? If so, what does that look like in your life?

3. What aspect of eternity do you look forward to the most? Why?

4. Do you believe that the stewardships of Earth are merely the beginning of the eternal work God wants to do in and through us? Assess your current stewardships in light of eternity.

5. What is the greatest revelation God has given you while reading this book? How has this changed your life?

ADDENDUM: VIRTUAL CHURCH

We have added the following two sections that do not directly address church related issues, but are societal challenges that will most certainly affect people in the church, and those we love. The information in the second section, My Robot?, discusses some challenging but essential subject matter.

PDA Addictions

Imagine yourself in an intense, even emotional, conversation with someone. As you reach the height of your discussion, his PDA (Personal Digital Assistant) rings and, to your complete surprise, he answers it! Seem familiar?

The first waves of relationship-killing behavior strikes close to home, revealing the sinister side of present technology.

A 2008 study of PDA use determined some troubling statistics about people and their virtual companions.[1]

- 87% bring their PDA into the bedroom
- 35% choose their PDA over their spouse
- 84% check their PDA's just before going to bed and as soon as they wake up
- 85% sneak a peak at their PDA in the middle of the night
- 80% check their e-mail before morning coffee
- 85% feel the PDA allows them to spend more time out of the office
- 79% feel like they can be just as productive out of the office as in
- 84% said the technology allows for more flexibility and time with family and friends

---

1 This September 2008 study was conducted via phone by STUDYLOGIC LLC, who surveyed 6500 workplace professionals with an individual income of $50K+, at least two business trips per year, and a Blackberry or mobile email device. Five countries, the U.S.—1,500 respondents—China, Australia, the United Kingdom and Germany, were polled.

- 77% said the PDA helps them enjoy life
- 62% "love" their PDA

Who would have imagined that such a simple, helpful electronic tool would be so deviously addictive? How many of you have unintentionally become ensnared in one or more of these obsessive behaviors?

If it is true that you have an inappropriate connection to your own PDA, remember the admonition of Jesus. "So if your eye—even your good eye—causes you to lust, gouge it out and throw it away. It is better for you to lose one part of your body than for your whole body to be thrown into hell. And if your hand—even your stronger hand—causes you to sin, cut it off and throw it away. It is better for you to lose one part of your body than for your whole body to be thrown into hell."[2]

Jesus stresses that if we give a dimension of our lives over to a sin or an addiction, we'd be better off to "lose" the one part than to allow it to infect and destroy our whole life.

My Robot?

At one point in history, people could never have imagined that families would just sit around TV screens merely watching actors carry on conversations.

When the TV became a normalcy, we balked at the fantastical handheld device that put Captain Kirk into direct mobile contact with Spok.

With cell phone in hand, I wonder what technology, that now seems ridiculous, will become part of our daily lives in the near future?

I believe the day of the life-like robot will soon be here.

---

[2] Matthew 5:29–31

Films like *I, Robot*, *Centennial Man*, and *A.I.* provide a glimpse into the not-too-distant world of human-to-robot interaction.

But the reality of robots in our future will have a further twist.

Human-to-robot contact will encompass physical, sexual, emotional and relational dimensions. On a purely physical level, the existence of sex objects is nothing new, but what is new is that it has burgeoned into a multi-billion dollar global industry.

On the emotional and relational plane, so many people have failed at human-to-human relationships, their need to connect on some meaningful level, even if it was with an inanimate android, is very strong. A person using fantasy to embrace imaginary possibilities is not novel. Adam and Eve did it in the Garden and millions do it every day on a myriad of surreal levels.

A woman went to her pastor asking for prayer. She told him that a certain character in a soap opera was in trouble and asked him to join her in a prayer. The surprised pastor responded, "But this person is not real!" She quickly answered, "I know, I know, but he really needs our prayers."

David Levy, president of the International Computer Games Association, and author of *Love and Sex With Robots*, says that by the year 2050 it will be commonplace for people to have sex with androids. "Robot sex will become the only sexual outlet for a few sectors of the population," he said in an October 2007 interview. "The misfits, the very shy, the sexually inadequate and uneducable. For different sectors of the population robot sex will vary between something to be indulged in occasionally, and only when one's partner is away from home on a long trip, to an activity that supplements one's regular sex life, perhaps when one's partner is not feeling well, or not feeling like sex for some other reason."[3]

---

3 David Levy has worked in the field of Artificial Intelligence since graduating from St. Andrews University, Scotland, in 1967. He led the team that won the 1997 Loebner Prize in Artificial Intelligence in New York.

During this interview, Levy gave us a futuristic glimpse into the warped thinking of some robotic pioneers. "The sometimes use of anthropomorphisms (attributing human characteristics or behavior to an object) was quite deliberate. I hope that in this way the reader will be led somewhat gently to the feeling that the robots of the future will, at least in some sense, be alive." Alive? WOW!

Levy continued, "…in terms of the outward appearance and behavior of robots, I am convinced that they will be designed to be all but indistinguishable to the vast majority of the human population." He went so far as to assert that, "…one of the great benefits of sexual robots will be their ability to teach lovemaking skills, so that men who do feel inadequate will be able to take unlimited lessons, in private, from robot lovers…"

I know some of you reading this will say that the possibility of this actually happening is absurd. But with the pervasiveness of STD's, AIDS, the threat of divorce, alimony, and other perils associated with human-to-human contact, additional forms of social interaction and bonding will be sought. Robotic companions will be pre-programmed to communicate in the specific ways most desired by their human counterparts. As experimentation with sophisticated and life-like robots takes place, human-to-robot soul-ties will be established. This will eventually lead to the wholesale acceptance of human-to-robot relationships in every dimension.

I am convinced that, unless there is a revival within the Western World, human-to-robot interaction on all levels will become completely acceptable within my lifetime. This is a staggering thought yielding civilization-destroying implications. Yet, barring divine intervention, I believe it will take place.

British Telecom futurologist, Ian Pearson, has said that robots will be fully conscious, possessing superhuman levels of intelligence by the year 2020. In a 2005 interview with The Observer, a UK newspaper, he humorously stated, "…realistically by 2050 we would expect to be able to download your mind into a machine, so when you die it's not a major career problem."[4]

Though there is nothing funny about the long-term tragic consequences of this de-humanizing and fully demonized human behavior, it will nonetheless become a future battlefield we will have to face. I am also confident that God will give us the wisdom needed to defeat this future enemy, "…lest Satan should take advantage of us; for we are not ignorant of his devices."[5]

---

[4] Smith D. 2050-and immortality is within our grasp. The Observer. May 22, 2005.
Available at http://www.guardian.co.uk/science/2005/may/22/theobserver.technology.
Last accessed July 15, 2009.

[5] 2Corithians 2:11

ADDENDUM: ETERNAL CHURCH

Called to Help a Persecuted People

I have already finished writing this book. Two editors and I are in the last days of the final proofreading of the chapters. Last night, while in the initial phase of forty days of fasting and prayer, the Lord awoke me around 4AM with an End Times dream about Israel. I have had precious few dreams either about Israel or about the End Times. Nevertheless, as I laid in bed and prayed, God began to speak to my heart about adding this section to the book.

Upon opening my computer to begin writing, I saw the History Channel had sent me an email with the heading: "What Will The World Be Like In 2012? Find Out Now!" It was advertising four videos: "Life After People," "Armageddon: Exploring the Doomsday Myth," "The Lost Book of Nostradamus," and "Nostradamus 2012" which discusses the prophecies of Nostradamus, a French apothecary and reputed seer who published collections of prophecies that have since become famous worldwide.[1]

Another email I opened was the "Verse of the Day"—John 12:12-13. The context for these scriptures is five days prior to Christ's crucifixion. The section is entitled, "Jesus' Triumphant Entry":

> "The next day, the news that Jesus was on the way to Jerusalem swept through the city. A large crowd of Passover visitors took palm branches and went down the road to meet Him. They shouted, "Praise God! Bless the one who comes in the name of the Lord! Hail to the King of Israel!"[2]

---

[1] www.en.wikipedia.org/wiki/Nostradamus

[2] John 12:12–13

ADDENDUM

This coming weekend, as our church continues an expository series on the Book of Romans, I am preaching from Romans 9:1–5, which states:

> *"In the presence of Christ, I speak with utter truthfulness—I do not lie—and my conscience and the Holy Spirit confirm that what I am saying is true. I tell the truth in Christ, I am not lying, my conscience also bearing me witness in the Holy Spirit, my heart is filled with bitter sorrow and unending grief that I have great sorrow and continual grief in my heart for my people, my Jewish brothers and sisters. I would be willing to be forever cursed—cut off from Christ!—if that would save them.*
>
> *"For I could wish that I myself were accursed from Christ for my brethren, my countrymen according to the flesh. They are the people of Israel, chosen to be God's special children. God revealed His glory to them. He made covenants with them and gave His law to them. They have the privilege of worshiping Him and receiving His wonderful promises, who are Israelites, to whom pertain the adoption, the glory, the covenants, the giving of the law, the service of God, and the promises; their ancestors were great people of God, and Christ Himself was a Jew as far as His human nature is concerned. And He is God, who rules over everything and is worthy of eternal praise! Amen."*[3]

Needless to say, having meditated on these verses, some of the most enigmatic in the Bible, my heart has been in awe. I can wrap my arms around laying down my life for someone I love. I can even imagine giving my life obediently for someone I don't know if God led me and gave me the grace. But what I cannot fathom is how Paul, the author of Romans, was willing to personally go to hell forever if it meant the salvation of God's beloved people, Israel. This is super-human love, and every time I think about being willing to do this, I have a brain freeze.

---

3 Romans 9:1–5

Before I share my dream, let me provide some personal background that has potential implications for what I am about to read.

Though I have visited Israel and been greatly impacted by her plight since becoming a Christian, I have more often than not been perplexed as to what my relationship with Israel should be.

Besides being born again on Israel's 24th Anniversary as a nation: May 14, 1972, other equally puzzling Israel connections have shrouded my life. My twin brother and I were born on February 23, 1949, and as I have contemplated it, it has frankly not been hard to imagine that we were conceived on Israel's birth as a nation, nine months prior: May 14, 1948. That was the day Israel declared its sovereignty and was immediately recognized by the United States and President Truman. My first Holy Communion as a young Catholic boy took place on May 14, 1955, Israel's sixth birthday. During my college years, I was the first non-Jewish president of my pre-dominantly Jewish fraternity.

But what is perhaps most perplexing of all was my father's relationship with Israel. As a Congressman, he had somehow cultivated a deep bond with this fledgling nation. I remember meeting the Israeli ambassador at a political dinner honoring my father, and when my brother Joseph and I were home from boarding school, my father asked us if we'd rather live in Rome, Washington D.C. or Israel. It was 1964, the year after President Kennedy had been assassinated, and Johnson had become President. My father had campaigned for Johnson in the 1960 election, and so when he came to power, options for my father's political career were put on the table, one of which was a position as Ambassador to Israel.

My most mystifying picture of my father occurred at a ceremony in the Rose Garden at the White House with President Kennedy, honoring the first President of Israel, Dr. David Ben Gurion. My dad was standing in-between Kennedy and Ben Gurion as the latter was given an award.

In any case, my father's health failed, and the opportunity passed. But Israel is certainly a part of our family tree. That said, I have done pathetically little to dig this prophetic well. Perhaps in the years to come I, and the persecuted Western Church will rise to assume a greater responsibility in befriending and interceding for Israel.

In my dream last night, a thousand Israeli soldiers were in a large building that was suddenly attacked by her enemies. As they attempted to flee, they found themselves surrounded and being slaughtered. I woke up with a great burden for their plight, and as I said, began to pray for them. I wish I were writing this section with a greater understanding of what it all means and what exactly the church's future responsibility should be toward Israel, but let me end this section with these provoking verses.

"And the day will come when I will cause the ancient glory of Israel to revive, and then at last your words will be respected. Then they will know that I am the LORD."[4]

"You will arise and have mercy on Jerusalem—and now is the time to pity her, now is the time you promised to help."[5]

"For Zion's sake I will not keep silent, for Jerusalem's sake I will not remain quiet, till her righteousness shines out like the dawn, her salvation like a blazing torch."[6]

"Let Israel hope in the Lord; for with the Lord there is mercy, and with Him is plenteous redemption."[7]

"So the angel who spoke with me said to me, 'Proclaim, saying, "Thus says the LORD of hosts: I am zealous for Jerusalem and for Zion with great zeal. I am exceedingly angry with the nations at ease; For I was a little angry, and they helped—but with evil intent." 'Therefore thus says the LORD: "I am returning to Jerusalem with mercy; My house shall be built in it," says the LORD of hosts, "And a surveyor's line shall be stretched out over Jerusalem."' "Again proclaim, saying, 'Thus says the LORD of hosts: "My cities shall again spread out through prosperity; The LORD will again comfort Zion, and will again choose Jerusalem."'"[8]

"Pray for the peace of Jerusalem: May they prosper who love you."[9]

---

[4] Ezekiel 29:21
[5] Psalm 102:13
[6] Isaiah 62:1
[7] Psalm 130:7
[8] Zechariah 1:14–17
[9] Psalm 112:6, NKJV

ADDENDUM

RECOMMENDATIONS: OTHER TITLES BY FRANCIS ANFUSO

Father Wounds—Reclaiming Your Childhood

As an abandoned and abused son, my soul suffered long-term destruction. But my wounded heart was exactly what God wanted to heal and restore. God can help you forgive the parent who hurt you. He wants to heal you completely and use you mightily in the lives of others!

FATHER WOUNDS

reclaiming your childhood

FRANCIS ANFUSO

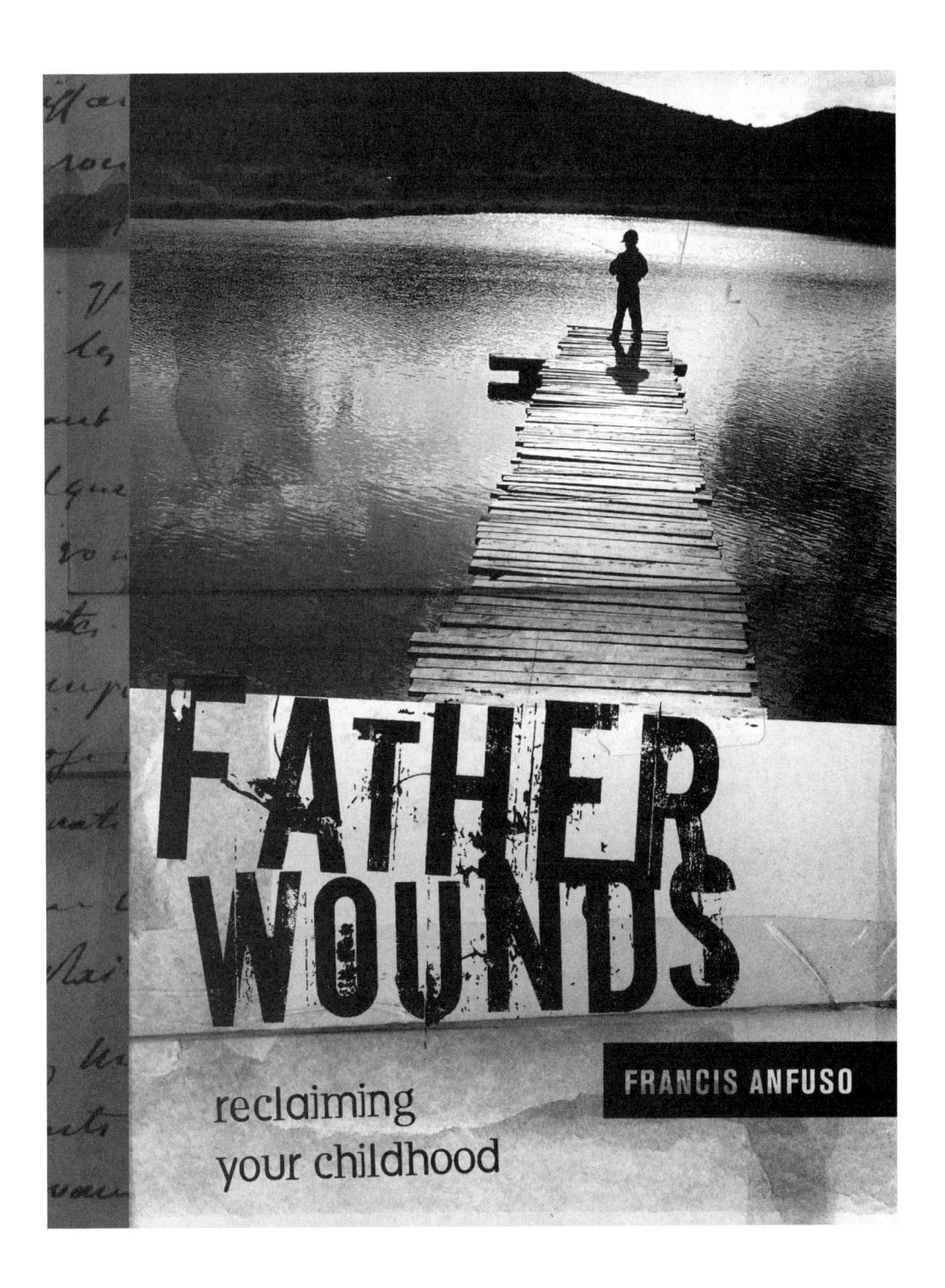

Perfectly Positioned—When Perspective Triumphs Over Circumstance

Our lives begin to be truly transformed when we stop asking God to change our circumstances and allow Him to change our perspective! Behind every challenging situation there is a loving God whose victorious perspective is far greater than the trials we face. The breakthrough you're longing for is just ahead!

Order books and audio books online at *www.rockofroseville.org*

PERFECTLY POSITIONED

when perspective triumphs over circumstance

FRANCIS ANFUSO

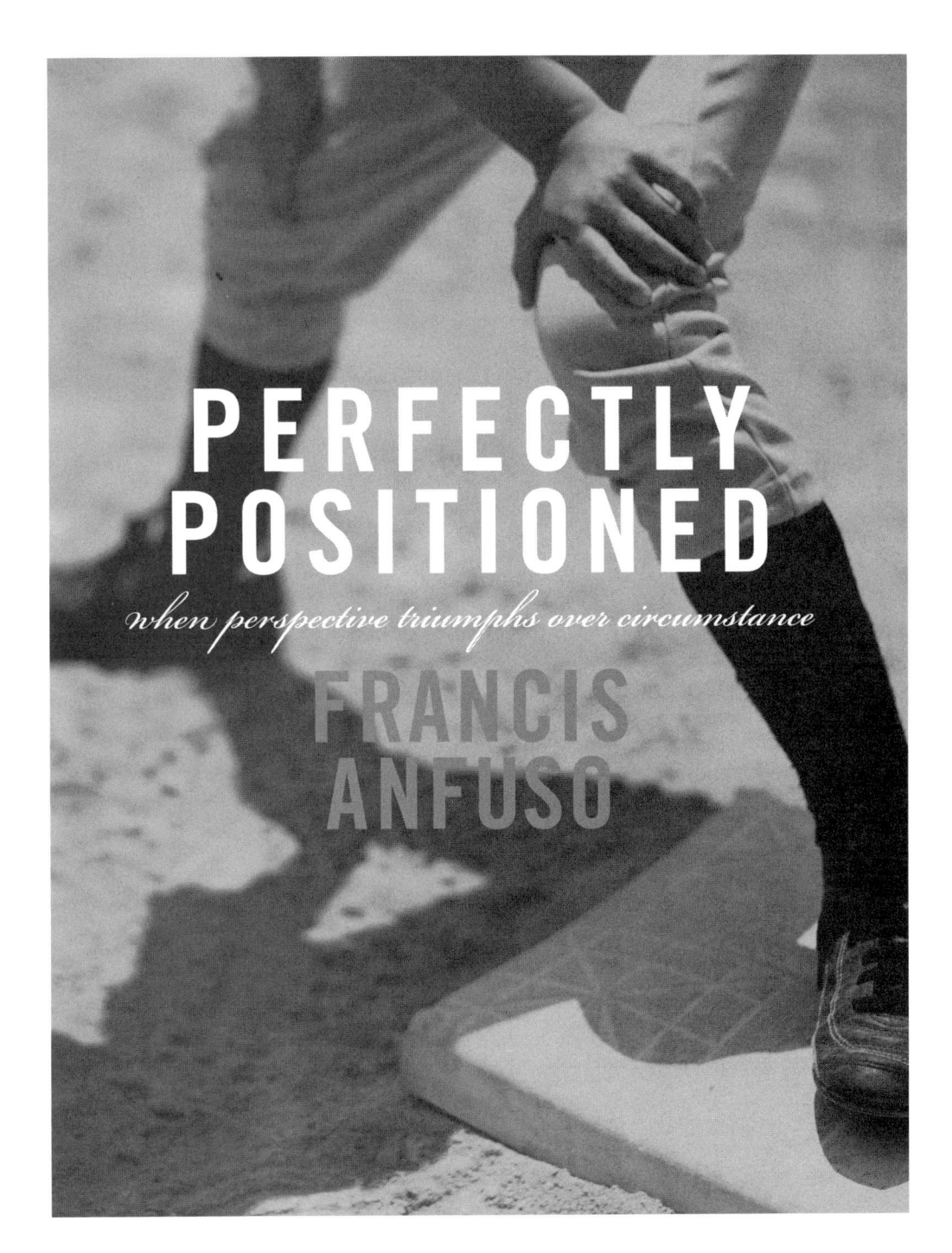

RECOMMENDED VIEWING

Rockspots

Find video clips of Francis Anfuso online at: *www.rockspots.tv.*